SPECIAL SUPPLEMENT
for PURCHASERS of
THE BEAT INFLATION STRATEGY

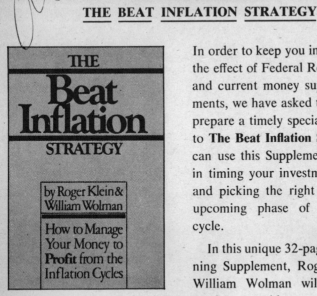

THE
Beat Inflation
STRATEGY

by Roger Klein &
William Wolman

How to Manage
Your Money to
Profit from the
Inflation Cycles

In order to keep you informed about the effect of Federal Reserve actions and current money supply developments, we have asked the authors to prepare a timely special Supplement to **The Beat Inflation Strategy.** You can use this Supplement as a guide in timing your investment decisions and picking the right asset for the upcoming phase of the inflation cycle.

In this unique 32-page profit-planning Supplement, Roger Klein and William Wolman will report and evaluate the latest Federal Reserve data, provide an analysis of the current stage in the inflation cycle, and offer specific investment strategy to help you build a winning portfolio of assets according to the principles set forth in this book.

To receive the current Supplement, simply fill in your name and address on the order form below and send it with your remittance of $2.95 to:

Simon and Schuster, Publishers
Dept. FE
1230 Avenue of the Americas
New York, N. Y. 10020

Please send me promptly at $2.95 per copy the Profit-Planning Special Supplement with current commentary on **The Beat Inflation Strategy.** I enclose $_____ in full payment.

NAME...

ADDRESS..

CITY...................STATE...........ZIP........

The
Beat Inflation
Strategy

Roger Klein and William Wolman

A FIRESIDE BOOK
PUBLISHED BY SIMON AND SCHUSTER

To Pat, Shayne, Anne and Ann

A Fireside Book
Published by Simon and Schuster
A Division of Gulf & Western Corporation
Simon & Schuster Building
Rockefeller Center
1230 Avenue of the Americas
New York, New York 10020
FIRESIDE and colophon are trademarks
of Simon & Schuster

Designed by Edith Fowler
Manufactured in the United States of America

4   5   6   7   8   9   10   11   12   13

Library of Congress Cataloging in Publication Data
Klein, Roger
    The beat inflation strategy.
        1. Investments.   2. Inflation (Finance)
I. Wolman, William, joint author.   II. Title.
HG4527.K55   332.6′78   75-12548
ISBN 0-671-22063-2
ISBN 0-671-23080-8 Pbk.

CONTENTS

Acknowledgments

Our list of specific acknowledgments is short. But four people worked hard to make this book better and get it out faster. Mary Mongibelli, now of the Economics Department of the First National City Bank, New York, is a real expert on monetary and investment statistics. Her unbridled passion for accuracy and consistency made life much more difficult for the authors but will make it much easier for the reader, whose representative she was in checking every fact and figure. James Saccento is the reason why the charts in Argus Research Corporation publications are so good. He is also the reason why the charts in this book help the reader rather than confuse him. Louise N. Fisher must be New York's best manuscript typist. Her speed and accuracy surprised even Simon and Schuster's longtime editors who knew the problems she was facing. Our agent Elizabeth McKee did everything a literary agent is supposed to do and did it well.

Excerpts from this book were published as articles in the April and May, 1975, issues of Time Incorporated's personal finance magazine, *Money.* The authors learned a lot from the way in which two practical *Money* men, managing editor William S. Rukeyser and senior editor Keith R. Johnson, approached the manuscript. The reader of the finished book benefits from some of their suggestions. The same is true of Sam Meyerson and Henry Robbins, our editors at Simon and Schuster.

Both Klein and Wolman were privileged to work in the Economics Department at First National City Bank, New York. Those who are familiar with the excellent work of that department will recognize the depth of our debt to our former colleagues. This is especially true of A. James Meigs, with whom we worked both at the bank and at Argus Research Corporation.

Our expression of gratitude to the women who are closest to us shows in our dedication. We undoubtedly enjoyed working on this book much more than they enjoyed having us work on it. Acknowledgments usually close with a line saying that the authors alone are responsible for all this book's deficiencies. This admonition is never frivolous and we too mean it seriously.

Preface

The world of high and volatile inflation that has existed since the mid-1960s will continue. But the investor need not be an inflation loser.

The Beat Inflation Strategy is based on the premise that inflation occurs in predictable cycles and that the investor can take advantage of his ability to predict these cycles to keep ahead of inflation.

When this book was written, the U.S. was experiencing double-digit inflation, stock and bond prices were tumbling and the markets for commodities and gold were strong. And a feeling was abroad in the land that these conditions would last forever. However, the Federal Reserve had already substantially slowed the growth of the money supply, and our analysis suggested that the inflation rate would slow down and that stock and bond prices would recover while gold and commodity prices would weaken. Looking at the broad sweep of developments in 1975–1976, a two-year period in which the rate of inflation was, in general, decelerating, this is, in fact, what happened.

This is consistent with our basic investment principle that there is no asset for all seasons but there is a season for all assets. Developments since late 1974 are also consistent with our belief that periods when the inflation is slowing down will be followed by periods when the inflation rate is speeding up. Monetary policy began to turn expansive in the spring of 1975, implying that the inflation rate would begin to move up in early 1977—a development indicating that investors who wished to stay ahead of inflation would have to change their portfolios. The investment environment therefore still appears to be the one described in the schematic diagram (Figure 8) on page 44. And the appropriate investment strategy is still the one summarized on pages 45 to 46 and expounded further in the rest of our book.

Investment books have a certain "timeless" quality—this means that they can deal with general principles but cannot give specific investment advice for specific time periods too far into the future. So, to aid the investor, a decision unusual in publishing was made: to issue periodic supplements to our book that set out for the reader the appropriate investment strategy for the upcoming phase of the inflation cycle. But the supplement goes further than that. It is, in effect, an easy-to-use workbook in which the investor can keep current on the status of the monetary growth cycle and the inflation cycle, and their implications for the prices of stocks, bonds, commodities and gold. Thousands of readers have written in for these supplements. By filling out the card at the front of the book or by writing directly to Simon and Schuster, readers of this Fireside edition can obtain the latest edition of our supplement.

Economic policy since the book was written confirms our view that inflation will continue to occur in predictable cycles, and that the investor who takes advantage of this fact will be able to achieve investment success.

Roger Klein
William Wolman
Summer, 1977

Introduction

Promises, promises, promises, that's all that people will get from those who have the power to end inflation. Congress hasn't done it and is not likely to. Nor is the White House. Nor is the Federal Reserve.

The wait for inflation to end will seem long, even compared to the vigil mounted by Gogo and Didi, the men in Samuel Beckett's play who were waiting for Godot. There is only one way to stop inflation: a government policy that deliberately sends the economy into a tailspin and jacks up unemployment. Governments will continue to promise an end to inflation for as long as they exist—it comes with the territory. But governments will not have the guts to maintain mass unemployment long enough to end inflation. Nor is anyone—including the authors—certain that they should.

Citizens of the Western world have been reasonably sure that they could get a job during the past decade. And jobs are likely to continue to be fairly abundant, at least compared to the pre-World War II economy. What is new is high and volatile inflation, and if you have a feeling that inflation has put you on a treadmill, and kept you there, you have plenty of company.

The plight of the typical American in his attempt to keep

11

up with rising prices is easy to document. In the United States inflation really took off in 1973. In just two years, 1973 and 1974, American families saw the purchasing power of their financial net worth—the value of their financial assets minus the value of their financial liabilities—drop by a cool $538 billion. This pushed their financial wealth below where it was in 1965. The average man has been working hard for the past nine years and doesn't have much to show for it.

But it doesn't have to be that way. Inflation doesn't destroy the country's wealth. It doesn't change the number of cars the country can produce, the number of houses that can be built, or the amount of food that can be put on the family dinner table. It doesn't destroy the national parks, mountain lakes, or seashore. There is nothing about inflation that changes America's capacity for providing the good life for its citizens.

This means that those Americans who feel inflation is making them poorer and their lives more meager must be doing something wrong. With net worth down $538 billion, millions of families are obviously in this position. There is a feeling of economic hopelessness abroad in the land.

But there is no reason why you have to number yourself among the victims of inflation. Gravity is a natural force and man has developed ways of making it work to his advantage. Similarly, inflation is not the bogeyman some people say it is. It is just another economic force. You are perfectly capable of making it work to your advantage.

This book will tell you how to do it. Inflation does not destroy wealth. Rather, like Robin Hood, rising prices take from some and give to others. Get out of your head the idea that you must be an inflation loser. It is just as easy to be an inflation winner.

When our friends asked us what kind of book we were writing, we replied, "A cookbook for those who want to beat inflation." The book gives simple directions on how to conduct every aspect of your economic life in a way that will allow you to keep ahead of rising prices; how to protect the income and pension benefits you get from your job; and more importantly, how to invest to beat inflation.

When you know how to win, the inflationary investment game is exciting and can be enjoyed to the hilt. When inflation is perpetual and volatile—and that is the way it is going to be—the investment game will provide much bigger rewards than when there is no inflation. But if you don't understand what inflation does, you are fated to be a bigger loser than when prices are stable.

If you are like most Americans, you have been one of inflation's losers. And if you ask yourself what you did to deserve this fate, the answer is sad.

For most American families it is simply that they have been behaving responsibly. In personal finance, the rules for responsible behavior derive from the "Puritan ethic" classically embodied for the United States in Ben Franklin's *Poor Richard's Almanack:* Work hard, be thrifty, don't borrow.

Poor Richard's rules are fine when prices are stable or falling. But they are a primrose path in a world of permanent inflation. This book will let you beat inflation, but the first thing you've got to do is to break all the habits you've learned from Poor Richard. Deep-six him.

Poor Richard's shadow will be hard to cast off, because it falls almost everywhere. He still blares at you from all sides: payroll deductions for series E bonds, automatic plans to transfer money from your checking account to a savings account that "pays the highest interest that the law will allow" (5½ percent or so), the New York Stock Exchange's Monthly Investment Plan, which allows you to buy shares in inflation-devastated companies at high brokerage commissions. All this is embodied in the slogan of the obscure, although important, Clyde Savings and Loan Association of Berwin, Illinois: "Put a little aside at Clyde." And what goes on in Drydock Country in the chic upper East Side of Manhattan is not much better, even though George Plimpton may be telling television viewers that the "in thing" to do is to save at the Drydock Savings Bank.

Although you've probably been wrecked by inflation, and are depressed about it, don't imagine that the so-called pros have done any better. The table shows how the 1973–74 inflation wrecked the money management pros, the alleged red-hot superstars of the investment management business. They're probably managing a good part of your pension fund if you're working for a big company and include the major New York banks. When it comes to managing money when inflation is rampant, David Rockefeller, chairman of Chase Manhattan, is in the same boat as most other people.

COMMINGLED EQUITY FUNDS
FOR EMPLOYE BENEFIT ACCOUNTS
Total Rates of Return—With Income Reinvested
(Years Ended 12/31)

	1974	1973	1972
Bank of New York	—23.3	—11.2	+19.7
Bankers Trust	—30.5	—28.4	+20.5
Chemical Bank	—20.6	—16.3	+11.4
Chase Manhattan	—27.3	—17.9	+ 6.5
First National City	—27.6	—18.3	+22.4
Irving Trust	—29.6	—18.4	+22.5
Manufacturers Hanover	—32.8	—20.2	+25.1
Marine Midland N.Y.	—11.9	—21.0	+11.8
Morgan Guaranty	—36.1	—20.8	+25.9
U. S. Trust	—34.1	—22.9	+21.9
Standard & Poors 500	—26.5	—14.8	+18.9
Dow Jones Industrials	—23.8	—13.6	+18.4

Morgan's 1974 figure is not from its commingled equity fund. It is the result for a $200-million General Electric Savings and Security Program. It is not necessarily typical of all Morgan pension trust and profit-sharing funds.

Source: New York Times, February 20, 1975

And so, for most of their lives, have been the authors of this book. We were trained in two of the better graduate schools in the standard tradition of economics. We worked for First National City Bank, one of the world's largest international banks, for Argus Research Corporation, one of the big names in the investment advisory business. But until recently we continued to think about inflation in all the wrong ways—Poor Richard's ways.

In fact, despite their radical chic, most American economists have been and are likely to continue to be Poor Richard's high priests. Their attitude toward inflation has been to sternly condemn it and to tell policy makers how to stop it. In our weaker moments we still do this. We abhor inflation and would like to see it end. But we now recognize that this moralistic attitude has caused us to fail in our most important job: advising people how best to cope in a difficult world.

Looking back at the inflationary years since the Vietnam War began, most economists would have to confess plenty of failures. First, their moralistic advice made the wish father to the thought. Because they wanted inflation to end, and kept telling the government how to end it, they began to base their practical advice and forecasts on the notion that inflation would end. But prices kept soaring; so the practical advice was lousy.

The fault does not lie with economics but with the moralistic approach that economists have followed. Practical economics has a lot to say about developing strategies for beating inflation, and we now know that we can best do our job by stating strategies as clearly as possible for all to see. We have cast out the window the inhibitions placed on us by the moralistic tradition of economics. We advise you to do the same thing. In the next decade everyone should emulate Dr. Strangelove: Stop worrying and learn to love inflation.

For you *can* beat inflation. And once you develop confidence that you can, life will be a whole lot better, because inflation will be a permanent part of the scene for as far as the eye can see.

John Kenneth Galbraith once said that writing is a colossal exercise of the ego. We feel that we ought to lay our egos on the line right now. Although we believe we have cast off the moralistic biases that warp the work of many economists, we also believe we bring to the development of a *Beat Inflation* strategy the best that economic analysis and research have to offer. Consequently, although we think we have written clearly, this book may be a little tough going in spots. But the reader can rest assured that what we have to say about a practical strategy to beat inflation will also find acceptance in the most rarefied of academic circles. We do not apologize for this; we think it is a plus. Whatever the failures of its practitioners, economic theory has much to say about what to do to beat inflation. It is still the best wheel around, and by far.

Although we agree that many economists with good credentials—economists who receive the applause of their peers —have fallen down, their mistakes are but as sounding brass and tinkling cymbals as compared to the idiocy preached by some investment advisers with a wide following. These advisers, the Johnny One-Notes of the investment world, counsel everyone to place their faith in something hard, such as gold, regardless of its price. They and their followers have had some successes in recent years. But the world of high and volatile inflation is no place for the simpleminded or the inflexible.

Our cookbook is not a casserole cookbook. The technique can't be learned in five minutes of quick study and then used over and over again. Much more like mastering the art of French cooking, Beating Inflation requires some study and effort and a subtle touch. But the payoff will be big.

1

Perpetual Inflation—
Many Causes, No Cures

Everyone hates inflation. At least, that is what they say. But elected governments cause inflation. They cause it not by giving people what they hate but by trying to give them what they want most: jobs, higher income and big increases in government benefits.

If governments weren't reflecting the strongest desires of voters, there would be some hope that inflation would end someday. But in almost every world capital, governments are responding to the deepest desires of the public. This is why inflation will continue to be high and volatile. It is also why you will have to learn to live with it, beat it, and even enjoy it. This is the only response for a rational man in an irrational world.

Although high officials claim their hands are tied, they always have choices open to them. But if you put yourself in their position you would make the same decisions. Suppose Mr. Gallup were to present you with the following: Choose between more inflation next year and one million more people on the unemployment rolls.

Unless you feel more secure than most people do, the odds are that you would gamble on inflation. Citizens don't have this conscious choice open to them. But some people in high places do. And when they make the choice they are only reflecting what the public wants them to do. The public dislikes both inflation and unemployment. But it dislikes unemployment even more than it dislikes inflation. If the Bill of Rights were to be rewritten today, job security would go right beside life, liberty and the pursuit of happiness.

It was not always so. Prior to World War II almost no one believed that he had an inherent right to a job. Prices went up but they also went down, so, on average, prices were essentially stable. Now everyone believes in his right to job security, and inflation is rampant around the world.

The impact of the change in attitude is illustrated in Figure 1, demonstrating the difference between the behavior of prices in the period before World War II and their behavior since World War II. Charts drawn for other major industrialized countries such as Germany, France, Japan and Great Britain would look very much the same. Before 1945, wartime inflation was inevitably followed by postwar deflation. After World War II, however, prices marched to a different drummer. They still rose during wartime, but didn't come down afterward. And after the United States pulled out of Vietnam, prices really exploded.

The reason for this difference is not complicated. The year after World War II, the U.S. Congress passed the "full employment" act, stating that the government would vigorously promote two essentially inconsistent goals—price stability and full employment. Under the prodding of the United Nations virtually every other country adopted similar legislation.

In practice, the goal of full employment has taken precedence over the goal of price stability most of the time. There have, however, been brief periods in which price stability has temporarily moved to the fore. These periods are crucial to the *Beat Inflation* strategy.

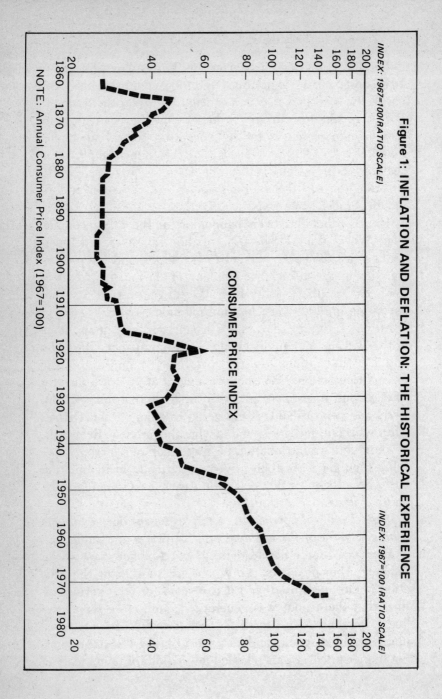

Figure 1: INFLATION AND DEFLATION: THE HISTORICAL EXPERIENCE

INDEX: 1967=100(RATIO SCALE)

INDEX: 1967=100 (RATIO SCALE)

CONSUMER PRICE INDEX

NOTE: Annual Consumer Price Index (1967=100)

The balancing feat envisioned by the Employment Act of 1946 and similar legislation in other countries has been enshrined by economists in a concept known as the trade-off. Policy makers operate in the belief that they can generate higher employment rates by accepting somewhat higher inflation rates. The problem is that the higher employment that results from inflationary policies only lasts for a while. In order to keep the unemployment rate permanently low, inflation must accelerate.

This is what has been happening in the U.S. economy since World War II. The U.S. inflation rate averaged 2 percent in the 1950s, 2.3 percent in the 1960s, and 6.1 percent thus far in the 1970s. The primacy of the full employment goal has similarly led other Western governments into accepting gradually accelerating inflation.

Although the inflation rate will move up and down, none of this will fundamentally change. The newspapers, the radio and TV will continue to carry government promises to bring an end to inflation. Don't believe a word of it. It is a disaster to base your investment plans on the hope that finance ministers and central bankers are going to change their stripes. They will continue to respond to what the public really wants.

The public wants inflation for more than one reason. They think they get more than just job security from it. Inflation has other attributes that make life easier if only temporarily. Quite a few other attributes.

It takes a lot of venom out of the argument over who gets a bigger share of the economic pie. If prices are stable, the workers and their union leaders can get a bigger share of the pie only if business gets less. When prices are rising the situation is more confused, and it can seem for long periods of time that the economy is generating much more for everybody. It seems to matter little that it really can't. It takes more output of goods and services to make the pie bigger, not higher prices. But it takes a lot less skill for union leaders and management to hang onto their jobs when prices are shooting up.

Inflation makes it easier to weather so-called liquidity crises, such as the Penn Central failure in 1970 or the difficulties of Franklin National Bank in 1974. When a well-known bank or company goes belly up, the Federal Reserve has two choices: either more inflation or more bankruptcies. The Fed can let nature and the relevant chapter of the bankruptcy law take its course or it can come riding to the rescue. In the good (bad) old days, it was thought that bankruptcies, like unemployment, were natural and inevitable, indeed, healthy. Today they are abhorrent. As a consequence, Washington lends money to Lockheed, rescues the commercial-paper market when Penn Central bites the dust, and becomes Franklin National Bank's chief supplier of funds, low-cost funds at that. Indeed, in today's world of Big Brother government it is only a few mossbacks like the editors of *The Wall Street Journal* (bless their hearts) who object. The frequency of these rescue operations will increase. Society always chooses inflation; people like it better than belly-up companies. Bankrupt companies have few employees.

Inflation is more palatable than gunboat diplomacy. When Teddy Roosevelt was speaking softly but carrying a big stick, a move by the Arab states to quadruple the price of oil would have been inconceivable. King Faisal would have been exiled to a modern-day St. Helena. And the U.S. Army Corps of Engineers would be pumping oil in the Persian Gulf.

But there is more than one way to get the oil. In today's world the creation of paper money can accomplish what gunboats used to. And what was true of oil in late 1973 can be just as true in future years for other raw materials whose supplies are controlled by the so-called less-developed countries. Just as inflation can be used to mask domestic conflict between labor and management over the distribution of income, so can it be used to mask international conflicts over the distribution of income and wealth.

Inflation makes the welfare state more palatable to those who aren't on the dole. A famous Italian economist of the early twentieth century, Vilfredo Pareto, observed a tendency for the distribution of income to be the same in all epochs of history and in all societies in the same epoch of history. Some dents have been put into the kind of income distribution curves that he drew—Pareto curves. In general, however, attempts to redistribute income from the rich to the poor have failed, for one reason or another, no matter where they have been tried.

Pareto's observations are relevant to the modern welfare state. When the New York taxi driver sees jobless people receiving bigger checks from welfare without working, he tends to rebel, or at least to strike. As a consequence, he fights to get more and succeeds, at least as far as the number of dollars in his paycheck are concerned. The fight of the white ethnic, urban working class to maintain its relative status in the face of rising welfare payments has been a force making for inflation.

Inflation seems to solve a lot of problems. It is little wonder that governments choose policies that are inflationary. But it isn't quite that simple, for, just as with heroin, it takes bigger and bigger doses to keep you feeling good—and if you don't get the bigger dose the withdrawal symptoms are severe, even deadly. When governments start trying to solve problems with inflation, it dooms society to accelerating inflation or severe withdrawal symptoms when the dosage is cut.

The money illusion explains why. To beat inflation you've got to understand the money illusion much better than other people do because if you don't you're going to be suckered by government policy.

Suppose that the government pretends to solve a problem,

say high unemployment. The classic way is to pump more money into the economy. Money is created by the actions of the Federal Reserve. When the Federal Reserve wants to increase the supply of money it orders its New York branch to purchase government securities. These securities are usually purchased from government security dealers, banks, insurance companies and other major financial institutions. What happens is simple but crucial. When some institution sells securities to the Fed it gets in return a check drawn on the Federal Reserve. When the Federal Reserve honors that check, the supply of money is increased. And Federal Reserve checks are honored immediately.

The process of money creation doesn't stop here. When the initial transaction is completed the financial institutions have more money and fewer securities than they had before. The money has to be put into use before it can earn interest, so the financial institutions will use it to buy other securities and to increase loans. When they do this the money supply rises by a multiple of the original Federal Reserve security purchase. Given the nature of the financial system right now, a Federal Reserve purchase of $1 billion in securities will increase the money supply by approximately $2.6 billion.

The effect of a surge in money is to jack up business sales volume. Companies hire more workers. But then comes the bad news, for as business gets better, prices start to rise, and usually faster than wages, which are pegged by longer-term union contracts. When prices rise faster than wages, the union natives get restless and start demanding and getting bigger wage increases. The source of their ire is a declining real wage, a situation where prices are rising faster than the number of dollars in the pay envelope, and purchasing power is declining. Workers won't stand for this. Either they get big wage increases right away or go out on strike and get them afterward. After that happens, the extra company profits that resulted from more money being pumped into the system vanish. Everyone's purchasing power is left about where it was before, but the price level is higher and the unemployment rate is back to where it was before the money supply was pumped up.

This is an example of the birth, life and death of the money illusion, and how government uses it to "solve" a problem in the short run. The whole process depends on a "money illusion" because at each stage of the process by which employment is raised somebody has to be fooled: the businessman into believing he will get permanently higher unit volume, the worker into believing that he will get permanently higher real wages. But the illusion dies, first as the worker realizes his purchasing power isn't rising, then as the businessman watches his unit profits eroded by higher unit wage costs.

The moral of this story—however immoral it may be—is that once a government gets hooked on inflation to solve problems, it can't kick the monkey without causing extreme pain. Initially the government made people feel better by pushing the unemployment rate down by inflationary policies, but the effect of a given dosage of inflation wore off. So to prevent things from going back to the miserable state at which they started, the government again has to jack up the inflation rate. And with nary a Phoenix House in sight. The money illusion also plays a role in all the other alleged "goodies" bought by inflation. Those who want to beat inflation will therefore find it prudent to count on accelerating inflation as their working rule. For just as the average inflation rate was higher in the 1960's than in the 1950's and higher in the 1970's than in the 1960's, it will be higher in the 1980's than it was in the 1970's. The *Beat Inflation* strategy is geared to the reality of accelerating inflation. The questions are: How much inflation? How steady an inflation?

2

The Inflation Cycle

Inflation will accelerate. But the path to higher and higher rates of inflation will be anything but smooth. The inflation rates will move ahead in fits and starts. There will be years when inflation accelerates and years when it slows down.

In a sense, people who really want to make money should thank their lucky stars for these gyrations in the inflation rate. They will create tremendous investment opportunities for those investors who have the right strategy for coping with inflation. A world in which inflation moves up and down will contain more and easier money-making opportunities than a world where inflation is steady or nonexistent.

Since governments create inflation, those investors who watch government policy closely will get ample advance warning of the amount of inflation that government will be creating. Whether its practitioners are willing to admit it or not, conventional investment strategy is based on the idea that prices will remain stable.

The *Beat Inflation* investment strategy, by contrast, is based on the idea that inflation will occur in predictable cycles.

The *Beat Inflation* investor must learn to understand these cycles and anticipate them. The major reason most American families have been on a treadmill since 1965 is that they didn't see inflation coming and therefore did little to guard themselves against its effects. You need never be caught unawares again.

The problem here is to separate those things that are ephemeral from those that will have lasting effects. Daily experience provides no clear-cut guide to the future of prices. And what it does tell you is often misleading. It is dangerous to form impressions about the future inflation rate from what happens on your job, from your visit to the supermarket or even from what you found out from Walter Cronkite. In fact, the successful investor will shut these impressions out. He will keep his eye on government policy. But in order to do this in an effective and efficient way the investor needs a framework.

The framework is provided by our concept of the inflation cycle. An understanding of this cycle is fundamental to investment success over the next decade. Ups and downs in the inflation rate will affect the prices of everything you own and can buy: stocks, bonds, commodities, gold, currencies and real estate. Some of these assets—such as commodities, gold and real estate—are superstars when the inflation rate is rising. Others, such as stocks and bonds, light the sky when the inflation rate is falling. The *Beat Inflation* investor will make money by shifting his investments from accelerating inflation superstars to decelerating inflation superstars depending on what stage of the inflation cycle the economy is in.

We will be publishing a periodic *Beat Inflation Supplement* that provides our current analysis of the inflation cycle and the suitability of various assets for the stage of the inflation cycle that lies ahead.* But nobody should buy a pig in a

* To receive this *Supplement,* simply fill in the order card in the front of this book, or write directly, enclosing your check or money order for $2.95 to Simon and Schuster, 1230 Avenue of the Americas, New York, N.Y. 10020.

poke, not even our pig. Consequently this chapter is devoted to an explanation of the inflation cycle, what causes it, how to predict it and what its effects on the economy and asset prices are.

Since what governments do drives the economy, the father of all cycles is the cycle in economic policy. The government policy cycle is rooted in the inflation/unemployment trade-off that was described in the preceding chapter. It occurs because policy makers shift with predictable regularity between measures primarily designed to reduce unemployment and measures designed to curb inflation.

Oliver Wendell Holmes once said that government policy always responds to the clear and present danger. Although inflation and unemployment both menace the politician, they never menace him equally. Sometimes inflation is Lucifer himself but other times—most of the time, in fact—unemployment is the Number One devil to be exorcised. Looking at economic policy since World War II, it is easy to break up the period into alternating subperiods when inflation or unemployment were Public Enemy Number One. Concentrating on the years since 1965, in Figure 2, when the Vietnam War heated up, a naked-eyeball analysis will show you that Washington was fighting unemployment from early 1965 to early 1966, inflation from early 1966 to late 1966, unemployment again from late 1966 to early 1968, inflation again from late 1968 to late 1969, unemployment again between late 1969 and early 1971. There was some vacillation in mid-1971. But in the election and economic-controls year of 1972, the government tried to slaughter unemployment, creating the need to fight inflation again in 1973 and 1974. In 1975 the focus of policy was clearly unemployment once again.

The first "fight unemployment" phase of the inflation cycle occurred in 1965, when the cost of a war was piled on top of spending for the Great Society. In late 1965 the escalating war costs were visible everywhere except in the official statements of President Johnson and his chief economic advisers.

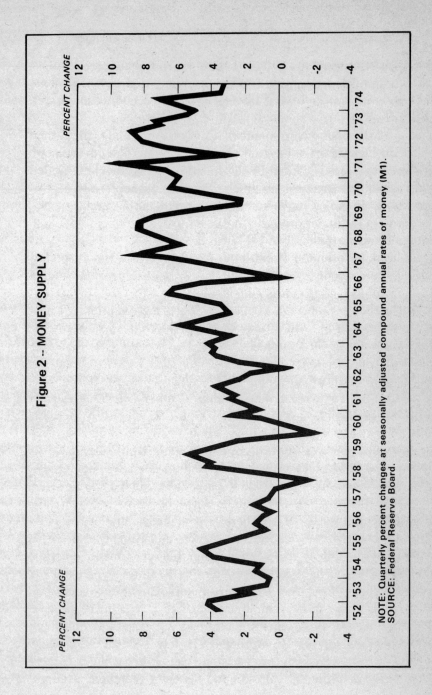

Figure 2 -- MONEY SUPPLY

NOTE: Quarterly percent changes at seasonally adjusted compound annual rates of money (M1).
SOURCE: Federal Reserve Board.

Yet the official working hypothesis of the Administration was (in its own language) that there was ample room for both more guns and more butter. The Federal Reserve let the quantity of money grow fast enough to accommodate the rise in spending, and employers began to scrape the bottom of the labor-market barrel.

By mid-1966 inflation started making headlines and unemployment was pushed to the back pages. Government responded in its typical knee-jerk way; it started to fight inflation. President Johnson proposed an income-tax surcharge but it took about a year for Congress to pass it. The Federal Reserve, however, moved more quickly and swung hard toward monetary restraint. These were the good old days when the money illusion was still something policy makers could count on. As a consequence, the inflation rate moderated rather quickly in response to the Federal Reserve's restrictive policy. The economy developed some symptoms of recession although the National Bureau of Economic Research, keeper of the seal in business-cycle matters, never officially labeled the period a full-blown recession. Unemployment, however, did rise.

This was enough to give policy makers the heebie-jeebies, particularly since Congress finally passed President Johnson's tax surcharge in early 1967. And many Washington economists felt that this would lead to fiscal "overkill." Therefore, policymakers switched to the other side of the trade-off—combating unemployment.

The Federal Reserve opened the monetary spigot wide, so wide that the deflationary impact of higher taxes could not be detected. And inflation again began to accelerate.

Consequently and predictably, President Nixon shifted policy goals to combating inflation in early 1969. It took over a year for these restrictive policies to begin to impact the inflation rate because the more policy cycles you have, the weaker the money illusion gets. The more often a country goes through policy cycles, the harder it is to fool people.

This time it took a prolonged period of anti-inflation policy and a real recession to get the inflation rate down. In fact, progress was so slow that on August 15, 1971, President Nixon pushed the panic button and slapped on controls to get the inflation rate down. But it wasn't too long before policy turned expansive once again. Since policy makers fear unemployment more than they fear inflation, the controls served as a veil under which economic policy again turned super-expansive.

Watergate was not the only thing that was done to influence the outcome of the 1972 election. Mr. Nixon and his Administration were taking no chances that high unemployment would cost him the election as it did in 1960. They pursued one of the most expansive monetary and fiscal policies in history throughout 1972.

This policy more than anything else was responsible for the accelerating inflation in 1973 and 1974. And freed of electoral concerns, Washington again turned its policy in a restrictive direction and remained generally restrictive for almost two years. It was only when unemployment really shot up in late 1974 that policy again shifted toward expansion. By the spring of 1975 policy was highly expansive.

The *Beat Inflation* investor can always tell whether policy is expansive or restrictive because the policy cycle is embodied in a monetary growth cycle. Anybody who is somewhat familiar with the work of economists knows that some stress monetary policy as the prime mover of the economy while others stress fiscal policy. The decibel level of the debate on this question has fortunately dropped. We have a preference for analyzing the investment outlook in terms of monetary policy. Specifically, we focus on the steps that the Federal Reserve takes to increase or decrease the monetary growth rate. The way we look at the world, tight money means a slowdown in the rate of growth in the money supply as occurred, for example, between late 1968 and late 1969.

Easy money means a speed-up in the rate of growth of the money supply as occurred in 1972. (See Figure 2.)

We believe that economic research indicates that changes in monetary policy have quicker and more easily discernible effects on asset prices than does fiscal policy—changes in government spending and taxes. However, almost all of the time, monetary and fiscal policy move together. This should not be surprising; when government turns expansive all policy wheels turn in the same direction. And when the brakes go on, all the engines go into reverse.

There is another, more esoteric reason why monetary and fiscal policy move together. When fiscal policy turns expansive, governments incur bigger deficits, which means they have to borrow more. Mechanically, there is no reason why higher borrowing by the Treasury must lead to a faster rate of money creation by the Federal Reserve. But in practice it does. Research by the Federal Reserve Bank of St. Louis shows that monetary and fiscal policy have moved in the same direction in 90 percent of all the quarters since World War II. One reason why we prefer to work in terms of monetary policy rather than fiscal policy is what happens the other 10 percent of the time. When monetary and fiscal policy move in different directions, monetary policy swamps fiscal policy and determines the direction of economic activity and asset prices.

A major technique, perhaps *the* major technique, in putting the *Beat Inflation* strategy to work is to spot changes in monetary policy. Figure 2 shows how monetary policy has swung during the post-World War II period. These policy swings are measured by changes in the rate of growth of the money supply. As we apply the *Beat Inflation* strategy in detail we will frequently talk about monetary *acceleration* and monetary *deceleration*. All that acceleration of the monetary growth rate means is that the money supply is growing faster than it was. For example, in December 1971,

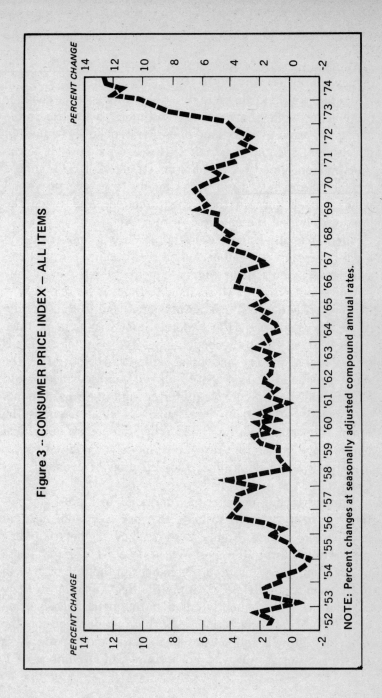

Figure 3 -- CONSUMER PRICE INDEX -- ALL ITEMS

NOTE: Percent changes at seasonally adjusted compound annual rates.

the money supply was 6.3 percent above the money supply in December 1970. By December 1972, it was 8.7 percent above that of December 1971. Clearly the monetary growth rate had accelerated during 1972. All that the deceleration of the monetary growth rate means is that the money supply is growing slower than it was. For example, as contrasted to the 8.7 percent growth in the money supply between December 1972 and December 1971, the monetary growth rate was only 6.1 percent between December 1973 and December 1972. Clearly the monetary growth rate had decelerated during 1973.

The monetary growth cycle, periods of accelerating monetary growth followed by periods of decelerating monetary growth, produces a cycle in output and an inflation cycle. The cycle in output is old hat. Everybody knows about the alternation between prosperity and recession. Economists have been writing about it for over a century. A decisive cycle in prices, however, is a phenomenon of the post-Vietnam years. It is the newness of this inflation cycle that has knocked conventional investment advice on its ear. As long as inflation remains high and volatile, the only way to increase your family's wealth is to follow the *Beat Inflation* strategy and play the inflation cycle rather than the output cycle.

The behavior of inflation over the last ten years provides the investor with a framework for understanding the inflation cycle. As Figure 3 indicates, there have been three distinct inflation cycles since mid-1965. The first one lasted from the third quarter of 1965 to the end of 1966. Its accelerating phase was very brief, covering the last quarter of 1965 and peaking in the first quarter of 1966. Its decelerating phase ran from the end of the first quarter of 1966 to the end of 1966. The second inflation cycle lasted from the end of 1966 through the first quarter of 1972. Its accelerating phase took three full years to work itself out, 1967 through 1969. The decelerating phase also lasted a long time, from the end of 1969 through the first quarter of 1972. The accelerating phase of the third cycle began in 1972, reached double-digit figures in mid-1973 and only peaked out in the fourth quarter of 1974. The economy was still in this decelerating phase of the inflation cycle in the first half of 1975.

The three inflation cycles over the past ten years illustrate four outstanding characteristics that will persist into the future and can therefore serve as the basis for the *Beat Inflation* strategy.

1.   The inflation cycle is preceded by the monetary growth cycle. Figure 4 brings together the money growth cycle shown in Figure 2 and the inflation cycle shown in Figure 3. The dotted line shows the rate of change for the consumer price index since 1952. The solid black line shows that the rate of change of the money supply lagged two years behind. The two-year lag simply means that the figure for the money supply that is plotted for 1974 is the rate that actually occurred two years earlier—that is to say, 1972. And so on. The resulting figure presents a revealing picture.

It shows that accelerations in monetary growth lead accelerations in prices and that decelerations in monetary growth lead decelerations in prices. The monetary growth cycle therefore serves as an early warning system for spotting turns in the inflation cycle. When an investor detects a decisive swing in the monetary growth cycle he can expect a definite turn in the inflation cycle. The turn in the inflation cycle will usher in a sequence of opportunity-creating events. Their consequences for the stock market, the bond market, the commodities market, and the interest rates obtainable on your short-term investments are described in subsequent chapters of this book. Taking advantage of them is what the *Beat Inflation* game is all about.

2.   The longer inflation lasts, the bigger the ups and possibly the downs in the inflation cycle. Figure 4 shows that the in-

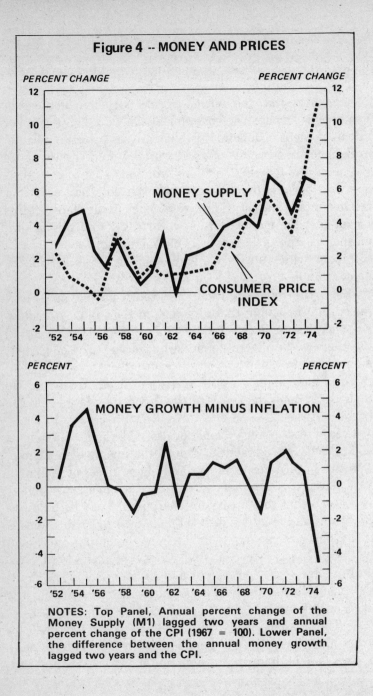

Figure 4 -- MONEY AND PRICES

PERCENT CHANGE
PERCENT CHANGE

MONEY SUPPLY

CONSUMER PRICE
INDEX

'52 '54 '56 '58 '60 '62 '64 '66 '68 '70 '72 '74

PERCENT
PERCENT

MONEY GROWTH MINUS INFLATION

'52 '54 '56 '58 '60 '62 '64 '66 '68 '70 '72 '74

NOTES: Top Panel, Annual percent change of the
Money Supply (M1) lagged two years and annual
percent change of the CPI (1967 = 100). Lower Panel,
the difference between the annual money growth
lagged two years and the CPI.

flation cycle has already become more volatile and that this is likely to continue.

Remember that the inflation cycle is rooted in the economic policy cycle. The government is always fighting either unemployment or inflation. In the early days of the inflation cycle, back in the mid-1960's, it was easy for Washington to get quick results when it swung from one goal to the other. This was because the inflation cycle started after decades of relative price stability. The experience with stable prices meant that the money illusion was strong. And this in turn meant that the government could eliminate a lot of unemployment with only a relatively small acceleration in the money supply.

When the money illusion is strong, people are easily fooled into believing that a change in their money incomes will make them much better off. But after inflation has lasted for a while they learn to be suspicious of a rise in their money wages or money profits because they know that when there is more money in their pay envelopes or their cash register, a rise in the prices of the things they buy is not too far off.

Therefore, the longer inflation lasts, the more stimulus it will take for government to reduce the unemployment rate. And this in turn means bigger and bigger doses of money in periods when government is bent on economic expansion.

It also means that an expansionary policy will be followed by bigger accelerations in inflation. And this in turn means that when government switches from the employment goal to the price-stability goal, the change in policy will have drastic effects, first on output and then on prices. In short, the longer the inflation cycle continues, the more volatile it is likely to become.

3. The periods in which inflation accelerates will be longer than the periods in which inflation decelerates. Policy makers hate both unemployment and inflation, but they hate

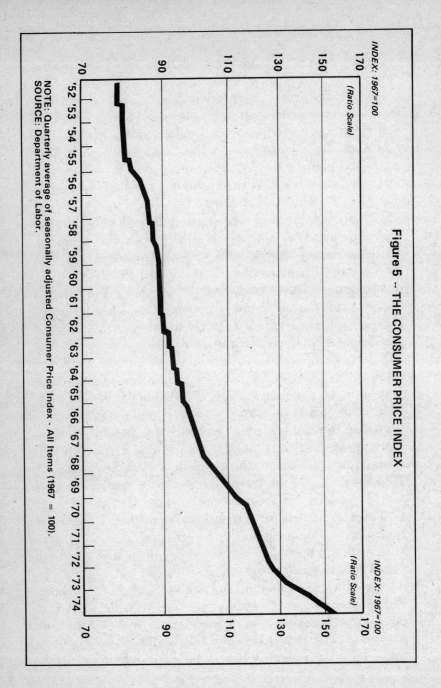

Figure 5 -- THE CONSUMER PRICE INDEX

INDEX: 1967=100

INDEX: 1967=100

(Ratio Scale)

(Ratio Scale)

NOTE: Quarterly average of seasonally adjusted Consumer Price Index - All Items (1967 = 100).
SOURCE: Department of Labor.

unemployment even more than inflation. As a consequence, policy makers are likely to panic more quickly when unemployment rises than when inflation gets out of hand. Furthermore, the longer inflation lasts, the quicker unemployment will shoot up when restrictive policies are adopted. This means that governments will lose their nerve soon after restrictive policies are put into effect, and they will switch to an expansionary policy. Expansionary policies will be in place longer than restrictive policies.

4.   Although inflation will be going through periods of acceleration and deceleration the inflation rate will trend upward on average. As the money illusion weakens, the government must increase the money dosage just to keep the unemployment rate steady on the average. And since a higher money growth rate on average will always bring a higher inflation rate on average, the rate of inflation will trend upward. This is illustrated in Figure 4.

Figures 2, 3, and 4 all show rates of change. Although these charts show cycles very well, they don't show trends very well. Trends show up very well in charts like Figure 5. This chart shows the level of the consumer price index drawn on a semi-log scale, where equal percent changes show up as equal vertical distances, so that a constant percentage rate of change shows up as a straight line. Since 1965 the line has been generally getting steeper. This means that the trend of the inflation rate has been rising.

However, it is almost certain that the extremely steep rise in the price line in Figure 5 that occurred in 1973-74 gives a misleading impression of the speed with which the trend of inflation is accelerating.

As we have described it, the inflation cycle is frightening, bringing as it does a volatile price level in the short run, coupled with accelerating inflation rates in the long run. But some perspective is required. It would turn out to be a grave mistake to identify the double-digit inflation of 1973–

1974 as the rate that was being produced by the monetary acceleration that occurred in the 1971–1972 period.

If you are going to be one of inflation's winners, you must be able to determine what the trend rate of inflation is, because your investment decisions are going to depend on your estimate. The biggest money-making opportunities will occur when there is a large difference between the current inflation rate and the trend rate.

As we have seen, the best way to get a grip on the trend of inflation is to keep your eye on what governments are up to as evidenced by the amount of money they are creating. Those who will beat inflation will keep their eye on the money supply.

Figure 6 shows the trend of money supply and the trend of prices. Two things stand out: (1) The trend rate of money-supply growth does not change very often, and (2) the money-supply growth rate is directly related to the rate of inflation. For example, in the 1950s the average money-supply growth was 2.6 percent while the average inflation rate was 2.0 percent. In the 1960s the money supply growth was 3.7 percent while inflation averaged 2.3 percent. Thus far in the 1970s the money-growth rate has averaged 6.2 percent and inflation has averaged 6.1 percent.

This kind of relationship holds up very well no matter what country you look at. Most of the Western countries keep honest track of their price levels and money supplies. And the money-inflation equation works well. Figure 7 shows the positive relationship between money and prices over twenty years in ten countries. The money inflation equation is an equal opportunity equation. It has no political biases, holding in communist countries, underdeveloped countries as well as developed countries, rich countries as well as poor countries.

For the United States, the trend rate of inflation is gener-

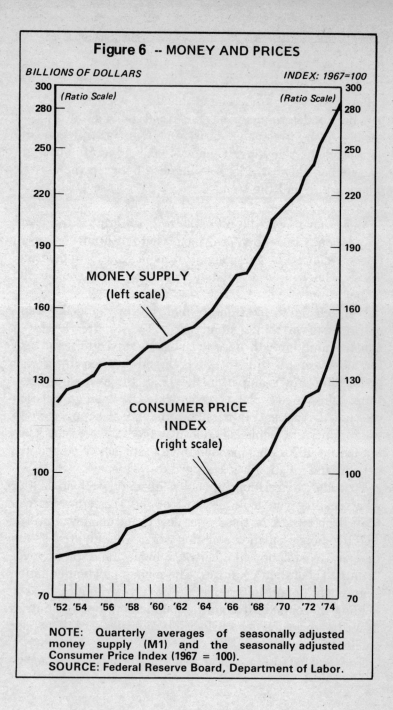

Figure 6 -- MONEY AND PRICES

BILLIONS OF DOLLARS   INDEX: 1967=100

(Ratio Scale)   (Ratio Scale)

MONEY SUPPLY
(left scale)

CONSUMER PRICE
INDEX
(right scale)

'52 '54 '56 '58 '60 '62 '64 '66 '68 '70 '72 '74

NOTE: Quarterly averages of seasonally adjusted
money supply (M1) and the seasonally adjusted
Consumer Price Index (1967 = 100).
SOURCE: Federal Reserve Board, Department of Labor.

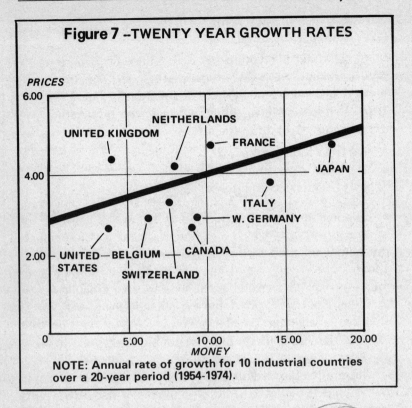

Figure 7 --TWENTY YEAR GROWTH RATES

NOTE: Annual rate of growth for 10 industrial countries over a 20-year period (1954-1974).

ally about 1 to 2 percentage points below the average rate of growth in money supply. This does not mean that it is 1 to 2 percentage points below the money supply growth rate in any given month, but rather 1 to 2 percentage points less than the money supply growth averaged over a three-year period. Using this rule, the trend rate of inflation is currently 4½ to 5½ percent because the money-supply growth rate has averaged about 6½ percent over the past three years. (See Chapter 12.) Since the inflation rate lags behind the monetary growth rate, the 4½ to 5½ percent trend rate of inflation will persist for some time. In fact, even if the extremely stimulative policies that have been followed so far in 1975 persist, it will be 1976 at the earliest before the trend rate of inflation increases.

All this talk of inflation rates of 4 percent, 5 percent, or 6 percent may seem like an overoptimistic prediction for a society that suffered double-digit inflation in late 1973 and 1974. But it illustrates that the trend rate of inflation can differ substantially from the actual rate and differ from it by a lot for quite a while. These are the times that those who put the *Beat Inflation* strategy to use can make the most money.

The actual rate of inflation can differ from the trend rate of inflation for several reasons. The first is the existence of the inflation cycle—which means that at any given moment, the actual inflation rate reported monthly will be moving above or below the trend line that describes the long-term inflation rate. The second is the existence of a phenomenon that has been recognized by statisticians for a long time: Random events cluster. It was this kind of cluster that boosted the inflation rate into the double-digit zone in 1973–1974.

This cluster that resulted in the double-digit inflation was a real lulu. It took an incredible number of negative events to make it. Jimmy the Greek would be ready to give you astronomical odds that it won't repeat itself. It was indeed a worldwide engine of inflation that even Rube Goldberg would have been hard put to design.

His contraption would have started with the dollar devaluation in 1971 and 1972. John Connally, the ex-governor of Texas, who was then President Nixon's improbable Secretary of the Treasury, would have been sitting in the Smithsonian Institution bullying the meeting of central bankers and finance ministers that ratified the devaluation of the U.S. dollar—a move that wrecked the U.S. price level by boosting the cost of foreign imports.

The scene would then have shifted to the Kremlin, where,

in a pre-election move to boost farm-product prices, the Nixon Administration sold wheat to the Russians at prices that even they couldn't refuse, draining U.S. farm surpluses and making the country vulnerable to an enormous surge in grain prices.

The next scene probably would have been set off the coast of Peru, where a thriving anchovy-fishing business had developed. It so happens that these little fishes whose fillets appear on the tops of salads are also used to swill hogs and feed cattle. They were a critical source of high-protein animal feed. Their disappearance from South American waters boosted the price of other high-protein feeds, mainly soybeans, into the stratosphere, and the price of meat soared throughout the world.

Then came the Arab-Israeli conflagration that gave the Arabs the opportunity to quadruple the price of oil and make the higher price stick.

The negative cluster of random events, combined with a worldwide boom in money-supply growth—mainly the result of the final futile attempt to prop up the dollar—blew the lid off the U.S. controls program, and double-digit inflation was on.

It took the painful monetary restraint of 1973 and 1974 to end it. By mid-1975 the inflation rate had subsided. But it had taken a steep rise in unemployment and a jump in excess capacity to do the job. But the signs of the next accelerating phase of the monetary growth cycle were present, since the aim of policy had turned to combating unemployment.

In a world of high and volatile inflation the investor who understands the anatomy of inflation is the one who will beat it rather than be victimized by it. Figure 8 is a schematic depiction of the anatomy of the inflation cycle. At each critical point in that cycle the asset mix that will beat inflation will be different, as subsequent chapters will show. The *Beat Inflation* investor must therefore always know where he

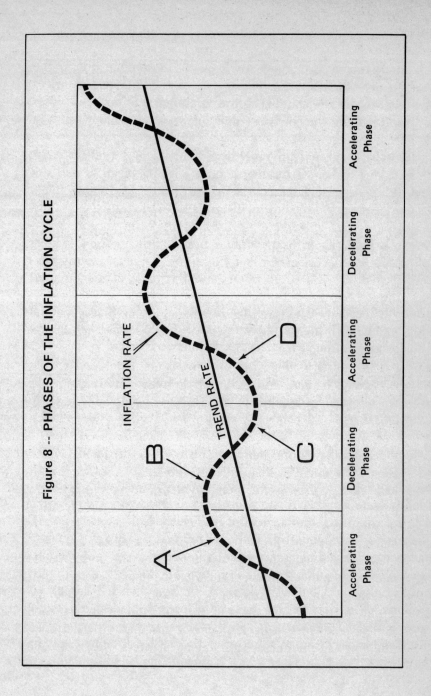

Figure 8 -- PHASES OF THE INFLATION CYCLE

is in the inflation cycle. He can do this at any time simply by getting his hands on the Federal Reserve Bank of St. Louis publications described in Chapter 12. These publications will provide him with the data to construct a real-life inflation-cycle chart which will quickly tell him where the economy is in the inflation cycle. The remainder of this book will tell him what investment moves to be making at each point in the inflation cycle.

For illustrative purposes we have picked four points in the inflation cycle. Inflation is going on at all times but each of the points requires a different strategy to benefit from inflation.

At point A, the actual inflation rate is still accelerating, but it is near its peak and well above the trend rate. The investor who has mastered the *Beat Inflation* approach will know why the stock market will be on its rump, interest rates will be high and bonds will be cheap. He will know why commodities and gold will have been bid up. But, more important, he will know what is going to happen next. At this stage of the inflation cycle, the *Beat Inflation* investor knows that the time has come to dump hard assets such as gold and commodities (Chapter 8), get into short-term money market instruments (Chapter 7) and get ready to buy paper assets such as stocks (Chapter 6) and bonds (Chapter 5).

At point B, the actual rate of inflation is decelerating but it is still above the trend rate. By this time the *Beat Inflation* investor is completely out of hard assets and is converting short-term money instruments into a portfolio of stocks and bonds ideally suited to take advantage of decelerating inflation.

At point C the inflation rate is below the trend rate and is in the process of bottoming out. The *Beat Inflation* investor is on the telephone to his broker, getting rid of his stocks and bonds, getting into liquid assets and thinking about the commodity and gold plays that will permit him to ride the accelerating phase.

At point D the inflation rate is below the trend rate but is in the initial phases of accelerating. The *Beat Inflation* investor is already out of stocks and bonds and converting his liquid assets to hard assets such as commodities and gold.

Poor Richard and the Protestant ethic have led the average American to draw a distinction between speculation (bad) and investment (good). One characteristic of Poor Richard's concept of an investment is that it is purchased and held for a very long time. Buying and holding was considered both ethically superior and more financially rewarding than in-and-out speculative trading. This may still be true with respect to any single asset. Trading in and out of stocks, for example, will probably make the broker rich but you poor.

However, Poor Richard's way to invest is the wrong way to invest in a world of high and volatile inflation. Over the entire inflation cycle no asset is ethically superior or more rewarding than any other asset. If you are going to make money over the inflation cycle, you must change the asset mix of your portfolio. The assets that will *Beat Inflation* at point A in Figure 8 will lose you money at points B, C, and D. There is no investment for all seasons, but there is a season for all investments.

3

How Inflation Transfers
Income and Wealth

Anyone who has ever played Monopoly knows that sometimes you win and sometimes you lose. But the way you would play would be different if you knew that all the prices —rents, the cost of the property, the fines you have to pay, and the rewards you get from Chance and Community Chest and the amount you get when you pass Go—double after every five times around the board.

Playing Monopoly in an inflationary environment would not change any of the physical aspects of the game. Mediterranean Avenue would still be the first property and Boardwalk the last. The houses and hotels would number the same and jail would still be jail and utilities would still be the same bad buys. But you would play the game differently. Because you would know the inevitability of inflation you would want to hold little in the way of cash, and borrow to the hilt in order to buy property and build houses and hotels. Moreover, your incentive to do these things would be greatest on the turn around the board just before the prices went up. Eventually you and your fellow players would develop a whole new set of rules for playing the game, and those who caught on fastest to the effects of inflation would be the biggest winners.

As with Monopoly, so it is with life. Inflation does not destroy the physical aspects of the game. But it does change the rules. Inflation does not necessarily produce disaster, but it does change who are the winners and who are losers. It does not destroy wealth or income, it redistributes it.

There are many views of inflation and its consequences that are contrary to our view. Predictions that inflation will destroy the game and the players along with it are common. This comes down to saying that society cannot develop tactics, rules, and strategies that will allow its members to live with inflation and still prosper. We believe, by contrast, that just as in Monopoly, the players in the economy will develop new ways of coping that will allow them to be comfortable when prices are rising. Indeed, there is plenty of evidence that help in adapting to inflation is on the way—cost-of-living clauses in wage contracts, Social Security benefits tied to changes in consumer prices, and variable-rate debt securities issued by bank holding companies and corporations. More help will soon be on the way.

The view that society will adapt to inflation is at the opposite pole from the one held by the gold bugs, the silver bugs, and the Swiss franc bugs, who see disaster behind every uptick in the price indexes.

The gold bugs should be regarded with disdain. It is true that the advice emanating from this intellectual underworld in 1974 was far better than conventional investment advice. The trouble, of course, is that although "crackpots" have their day, their pots are indeed cracked—the intellectual and factual underpinnings of their arguments simply don't hold water. The most obvious case is gold. Gold bugs, in general, counsel a strategy of either holding gold or the stocks of gold-mining companies regardless of their current price.

The reader should be wary of these Johnny One-Notes in the investment community. Under circumstances that could easily be foreseen (for example, a decelerating period of in-

flation like the one between points B and C in Figure 8),
nothing could be more disastrous than the buy-and-hold
strategy recommended by gold bugs or any other one-asset
bugs. Like any commodity, gold is an asset that will fare
best in the accelerating phase of the inflation cycle. See
Chapter 8, "When Commodities Beat Inflation." The key to
profiting from permanent inflation—and that is what we are
going to have—is a flexible investment policy that plays no
favorites among assets. Each asset will have its season. And
the *Beat Inflation* investor will move in and out of each
asset based on his assessment of its merits for each stage in
the inflation cycle.

WHERE INFLATION DOESN'T MATTER

Inflation will do no systematic damage to your chances to
enjoy the good things in life, just as it didn't destroy the
Monopoly board. This means that you can have more of
everything as you progress in your chosen career path.

In order to always understand how well off you are, you
must be aware of the distinction between the changes in the
number of dollars you report to the IRS every year and what
those dollars can actually buy.

The real Adam Smith, who made his reputation from *An
Inquiry Into the Nature and Causes of the Wealth of Nations*,
published in 1776, clarified this distinction once and for all.
The "real" wealth of nations or individuals, he said, must be
measured by the quantities of goods and services that they
can command. Modern-day economists describe changes in
these quantities as changes in "real" magnitudes, "real" income, "real" wealth, "real" wages and so on. The characteristic of these real magnitudes is that they do not necessarily
go down when prices rise. This is why inflation can be enjoyed rather than feared.

To improve your standard of living, you must increase your money income faster than prices are going up. What is true for the individual is also true for the country as a whole. The government spends a great deal of money providing the tools for drawing a distinction between changes in money values and changes in real values. Indeed, all the price indexes that the government puts out and you read about can be used for this purpose. For example, suppose the amount of money spent on automobiles rose by 10 percent in one year. At the same time, the Bureau of Labor Statistics reports that auto prices jumped by 10 percent over the same period. This means that the number of cars sold was unchanged. Or, in other words, there was no "real" growth in auto sales. And what is true of autos is true of everything else; when you adjust changes in money values for changes in prices—economists call this process deflating—the number you come up with is a "real" number: personal income divided by a measure of consumer prices is called "real" income, and wealth divided by an index of asset prices is called "real" wealth.

The basic finding of economic research spanning many centuries and many countries is that there is no fixed relationship between the rate of inflation and the growth in real income. In general, some countries have had high inflation and high real growth (Japan and Brazil are conspicuous examples) while others have had high inflation and low real growth (Italy and the United Kingdom are examples). Cases can also be cited for countries with low inflation and low real growth and low inflation and high real growth.

Given all the uncertainties in the world and the large errors made by forecasts, the prospects for the United States seem to be for high and permanent inflation and somewhat slower real growth than was chalked up in the 1960s. Looking at the years through 1979, we foresee a real growth rate of 3.5 percent, somewhat slower than the 4.3 percent that existed in the 1960s. For what comfort it provides, our forecast is not too different from the other forecasts included in a recent survey of long-term forecasts conducted by the economics department at RCA. Of the 12 forecasts included, the median growth rate forecast was 3.9 percent, the high 4.6 percent, and the low 2.9 percent. Remembering the wonderful world of compounding, this leaves plenty of room in which you can increase your standard of living.

Many readers may find the idea that inflation need not interfere with your chances of enjoying the good life somewhat hard to digest, in light of the horror stories and books now being written about inflation. Yet a little bit of introspection and observation shows that indeed it doesn't interfere.

First, consider how you yourself responded to the 1973–74 double-digit inflation. Economists have known, since Adam Smith's time, that a nation's growth rate is determined mainly by the character of its people and the quality of their education and by the increase in the number of hours worked by its labor force.

If you are like most other people, the odds are that you worked just as hard and maybe even harder in the face of accelerating inflation. A survey of psychologists conducted by *The New York Times* in the summer of 1974, a period of double-digit inflation in the United States, showed that inflation per se was having little impact on people's actual behavior although it was obviously high on the list of personal gripes. And when it comes to growth, it is not what people gripe about, but how they act, that counts.

The United States is not unique in this respect. The Japanese have had a high inflation rate for some time now but have not abandoned the work ethic. By the same token, the Germans and the Swiss have combined hard work with relatively low inflation rates. Even internationally, it is not the rate of price increase but other more fundamental characteristics, such as population growth, the rate of technological advance, and the level of education, that decide how fast the country's standard of living improves.

There is an important exception to this rule of the non-importance of inflation. Many people's perceptions of the horrors of inflation are based on a small sample of highly unusual cases of hyperinflation: the great inflation in the Confederate states during the Civil War, the inflation in the twenties, particularly in the Weimar Republic in Germany and Austria and Hungary, and the inflation in continental Europe after World War II. In each of these cases prices rose so rapidly and economic activity became so disorganized that real output tumbled. The common characteristic of these inflations is that they were enormously high by any standard. Thus, in his classic study of hyperinflation,* Professor Phillip Cagan of Columbia University and the National Bureau of Economic Research did not characterize an inflationary environment as "hyper" unless prices rose by at least 50 percent per month. In fact, most of the cases he studied exceeded this minimum figure. In Germany, for example, in 1923 prices rose by a factor of 100 billion in one year. This amounts to a doubling of prices every two weeks. The same kind of thing occurred in Greece in 1944, in Poland in 1923, in Russia in 1921–23 and in Hungary in 1923 and again in 1946. Cagan reports that the Hungarian inflation of 1946 saw prices doubling on the average every two or three days to a factor of about 10 with 26 zeroes after it in about one year.

As long as inflation falls far short of these multi-digit figures (28 digits in the case of the Hungarian inflation in 1946), high real growth is possible even though inflation is extremely high by the standards of U.S. history. Brazil, for

* See Professor Cagan's "The Monetary Dynamics of Hyperinflation" in *Studies in the Quantity Theory of Money,* Milton Friedman, editor, University of Chicago Press, 1956.

example, where inflation is running between 15 to 20 percent, has a real growth rate that is among the highest in the world. Japan, another fast-growth economy, has had much higher inflation rates than the United States.

Inflation should not be taken as a cause for despair, since income will continue to grow in any situation that falls short of hyperinflation for the United States or the world. Therefore, the practical question for the reader is how to position himself for the kind of inflation that is to come. To do this the reader must understand how inflation transfers income and wealth. From this will flow the strategy that will enable him to be one of inflation's big winners.

How Inflation Is Important

Irrelevant to real growth as it usually is, inflation does have enormous impact on the distribution of income and wealth. Like the inflation cycle, the process by which inflation transfers income and wealth is a key element of the *Beat Inflation* strategy. It will be discussed from three separate points of view. First of all we will show what the transfers are: in short, who are the winners and who are the losers. Second, we will describe why the transfers take place. Third, we will nail down the lessons to be learned by analyzing simple balance sheets to show how you can position yourself in terms of your assets and liabilities to beat inflation. Some people will be winners and others will be losers. What happens to you will be determined by your actions or inactions.

The rule for ending up in the winners' circle is to be on the right side of four kinds of transfers:

1) *The transfer of wealth from creditors to debtors.* Here it is your net position that is crucial. If your assets valued in dollars, such as cash, savings deposits and bonds, exceed

your liabilities valued in dollars, such as bank loans and mortgages, you are a net monetary creditor. You are hurt by inflation. If your assets valued in dollars are less than your liabilities valued in dollars you are a net monetary debtor. You gain by inflation.

Both Polonius ("Neither a borrower nor a lender be") and Ben Franklin were wrong; you *have to* be a borrower. But walk, don't run, to your nearest bank; the funds must be invested in the right portfolio, one that is designed to take advantage of inflation.

2) *A transfer of income from those who work in industries and professions where prices and wages are rising slowly to those who work in areas where prices and wages are rising more rapidly.* Early in this century the U.S. Department of Agriculture invented the idea of a parity index. This index measures the prices received by farmers and compares it to the prices paid by farmers. Since that time, U.S. farmers have used the index to box Congress and the President about the ears every time their relative position deteriorates, that is to say, every time inflation transfers purchasing power away from them. Those who will beat inflation must have a good subjective notion of their own parity position. They then must take the kinds of action that will at the least prevent their parity index from declining, and, ideally, make it rise.

This point is important. It is the only way to avoid getting trapped by the money illusion. In your own personal life the money illusion is the failure to recognize that while your wages and income from investments may be rising, so are the prices that you are paying to stay alive. A readily understood example is a man who is offered a transfer from Biloxi, Mississippi, to New York, New York. He may be offered a much higher salary; but he must make sure that his expenses do not rise by a higher percentage if he is to benefit. Many more subtle examples will be provided later, but the concept is the same. Purchasing power is what matters.

3) *A transfer of wealth to those who invest in assets whose prices go up faster than the general price level from those whose assets go up less rapidly than the general price level.* In the inflation that occurred in 1973 and early 1974, commodity prices in general were clearly the star price performers; common stocks laid the biggest egg. In finding the right vehicle at a given moment in time, be especially aware of those Johnny One-Notes who are always fiddling on the same string, no matter what that string may be: gold, land, Swiss francs, common stocks, art, or anything else.

4) *A transfer of wealth and income to those who correctly foresee the future inflation rate and take advantage of their foresight.* Those who can foresee what the inflation rate will be are in a position to benefit from the transfers described above. They will buy the right assets, be in the right industries, and arrange their balance sheet correctly.

There are two basic approaches to this wealth-and-income transfer. One approach is defensive-conservative, while the other is risky-aggressive but also potentially the most rewarding. The conservative hinges on what has come to be known as indexing. Under this approach, the idea is to neutralize inflation, i.e., to merely keep up with inflation. The strategy is to tie all income receipts and payments to some measure of the change in the general price level—the consumer price index, for example. Obviously the choice is up to you, but if you really want to make inflation work in your favor, the risky-aggressive approach is your cup of tea. But it means that you are going to have to form your own ideas about the speed of increase of the general price level, as well as determining what specific prices will rise the fastest.

The wealth and income transfers that accompany inflation are complex and are the subject of a technical body of economic literature about which those who will *Beat Inflation* need not worry too much. The basic idea is that money is a veil. What really counts, as we have seen, is real income and real wealth: what your income and wealth can buy in physical goods and services. Money, by contrast, is a medium of exchange which facilitates an efficient transfer of real income and real wealth. It does not become any more productive when prices go up; indeed, in some sense its productivity declines because each existing dollar represents a smaller fraction of total real income and total real wealth.

When inflation occurs, physical wealth is worth more in terms of money. For example, as inflation has accelerated, the value of your home has gone up with it, because it is more expensive in terms of dollars. But the claim against this physical, or hard, asset, probably a mortgage, does not change in value. You still owe the same number of dollars, but those dollars purchase less. Thus the homeowner's net worth—the difference between assets and liabilities—has increased. This is the way that inflation works to transfer wealth from net monetary creditors—in this case the owner of the mortgage—to net monetary debtors—in this case the owner of the house. All wealth transfers occur in this manner.

Income transfers are much simpler to see. Again, keep the parity index in mind. It is not hard to see that those who are sellers in markets where prices are rising most rapidly because of inflation will come out ahead.

Finally, those who are able to guess correctly about the future path of inflation will benefit at the expense of those whose guesses are not as good, because those who are correct are simply going to be able to choose the right industries, write favorable contracts, and bunch their borrowing and lending decisions in periods when the terms are most favorable. Above all, they will make the right investments.

THE ARITHMETIC OF WEALTH TRANSFERS

Readers who never liked bookkeeping can feel free to move on to the next chapter, but those who would like to nail down the lesson about how inflation transfers wealth should take a look at the following example showing why it pays to be a net monetary debtor, and why it's dumb to be a net monetary creditor when inflation is rife. Let's look at the balance sheets of three people: one a net monetary creditor, one neutral (monetary assets equal monetary liabilities), and one a net monetary debtor.

Mr. Net Creditor's balance sheet looks like this before inflation starts. He is a net creditor because his monetary assets, cash in this example, exceed his monetary liabilities, a mortgage in this case. In all our examples, the house is a "real" asset.

Mr. Net Creditor

Cash	10	Mortgage	5
House	10	Net Worth	15

Net worth is the difference between the dollar value of your assets and the dollar value of your liabilities and is a measure of how rich you are.

Mr. Net Creditor's net worth is 15: his assets (Cash, 10, and House, 10, for a total of 20) minus his liabilities (Mortgage 5). If prices, including the prices of physical, or hard, assets—houses—double, Mr. Net Creditor's balance sheet looks like this:

Mr. Net Creditor

Cash	10	Mortgage	5
House	20	Net Worth	25

This man's net worth has increased from 15 to 25. So far so good. But net worth has not doubled as prices did. This man has fallen behind in the inflation race. The purchasing power of his net worth (wealth) has been reduced by inflation.

Mr. Neutral's balance sheet looks like this, before inflation starts. He is neutral because his monetary assets equal his monetary liabilities.

Mr. Neutral

Cash	5	Mortgage	5
House	10	Net Worth	10

A doubling of prices has this effect on his balance sheet:

Mr. Neutral

Cash	5	Mortgage	5
House	20	Net Worth	20

This man's net worth has increased from 10 to 20. He has exactly kept pace with inflation. The purchasing power of his net worth (wealth) has stayed the same.

Mr. Net Debtor's balance sheet looks like this. He is a net debtor because his monetary assets are less than his monetary liabilities.

Mr. Net Debtor

Cash	3	Mortgage	10
House	12	Net Worth	5

When prices double, his balance sheet looks like this:

Mr. Net Debtor

Cash	3	Mortgage	10
House	24	Net Worth	17

This man's net worth has increased from 5 to 17. When net worth more than triples while prices only double, inflation has been beaten. The purchasing power of his net worth (wealth) has risen. He has been on the right side of the inflation-induced wealth transfer.

Notice that you don't have to be on the verge of bankruptcy to be a net monetary debtor. You can have cash, but you want a large portion of your assets to be physical, or hard, assets. As a matter of fact, you can get tremendously rich and still be a net monetary debtor. In our example, Mr. Net Debtor's net worth has tripled, but he is still a net monetary debtor, still positioned to benefit from more inflation. Most people who get and stay rich in the years ahead will have balance sheets that are leveraged this way. Their assets will primarily be composed of investments whose prices rise at least as fast as the general price levels at each stage of the inflation cycle. Cash does not fit into this group of inflation-benefiting assets because a dollar is a dollar is a dollar. And the purchasing power of a dollar shrinks with inflation. On the liability side you take the opposite tactic. Liabilities should be fixed in terms of the number of dollars owed so that they do not increase when the general price level rises. Mortgages or other IOUs generally fit this bill. The purchasing power you must surrender to honor them shrinks with inflation.

The principles that apply in our simple examples also apply in the real world. No matter how complex their balance sheets, net monetary debtors are the ones who will win because of the principles just illustrated. There are, of course, more complex effects of inflation on balance sheets that have entries for depreciation and inventories. These have important implications for your investment decisions and your common stock choices. They are covered in Chapter 6.

4

Investing to Beat Inflation

Those who will beat inflation will put their chips on those investments that are on the right side of the wealth and income transfers that come as a result of inflation. They will be on the right side of the transfer of wealth from net creditors to net monetary debtors: of the transfer from those who do not anticipate the inflation rate correctly to those who do; of the transfer from those industries where prices rise slowly to those industries where prices rise more rapidly.

We have looked at a large number of portfolios ranging from those held by people with normal income and wealth to the ones held by the very rich. Very few are structured to take advantage of inflation. In a world of perpetual high and cyclical inflation, most portfolios are a jumbled mess. The odds are that they contain some burned-out growth stocks, bonds that have a market value one half their redemption value, passbooks to an almost 5½ percent savings account—and, typically, the inflation-hedge portion of the portfolio includes some gold stocks bought when gold was at its peak.

Nor does it matter much whether your portfolio was created on your own or by some institution that has a big name, a fancy office and a lot of professional money managers running around. The big have fallen as hard as the small, as the table in the introduction listing the performance of New York City bank pension accounts illustrates. (See page 14.)

Obviously, if you were to walk into the upholstered offices of the money managers in these banks today with your money in your pocket they would balance these dreadful performances with a somewhat better showing over the previous five years. But press them and you will find out that they did not, and still do not, have portfolios designed to beat inflation.

This is not to say that the kind of conventional wisdom that guides the work of the professional portfolio managers should be thrown out the window in an inflationary world. In fact, many of the principles that they talk about, such as diversification and efficient portfolios, cannot be ignored. But as the authors now recognize after some painful experiences, the standard rules of investment must be applied differently in an inflationary environment than in an atmosphere in which prices are stable. They must be adapted to take advantage both of the inflation cycle and of the wealth and income transfers that it brings.

The primary focus of investment analysis has been to find undervalued assets to buy and overvalued assets to sell. We agree with this approach. Indeed, the search for undervalued and overvalued situations is not the reason for the poor investment performance since the inflation cycle got started. Instead, the problem has been failure to recognize that the inflation cycle has changed the criteria for spotting overvalued and undervalued situations. Conventional investment analysis has simply not taken account of the inflation cycle and its impact on asset prices. When looking at an asset, the fundamental consideration of the *Beat Inflation* investor should be what the inflation cycle does to the potential return from investing in that asset. The *Beat Inflation* investor concentrates on the impact of the inflation rate on asset prices more than anything else.

This book is designed to help you pick those assets that are potentially overvalued or potentially undervalued for each stage of the inflation cycle. Accelerating inflation will destroy the value of some assets and enhance the value of others; decelerating inflation will enhance the value of some assets and destroy the value of others. There is no asset whose value is immune from inflation.

The details of how and why inflation alters asset values is what the remainder of this book is all about. The method, for example, would have shown you:

(1) That gold was overvalued in the spring of 1974. Looked at on a long-term basis, its price had risen far faster than prices in general and it was due for a fall. And fall it did until the autumn of the same year when Congress passed legislation allowing Americans to hold gold. And when this happened we again pointed out the overvaluation of gold for the upcoming stage of inflation cycle and gold again fell.

(2) That bonds were undervalued in the early fall of 1974. The expected inflation rate incorporated into bond yields was too high for the upcoming stage of the inflation cycle, a conclusion reached by the methods described in Chapter 5. Bond yields fell and bond prices rose and those who invested in them *Beat Inflation.*

(3) That commodities were overvalued in the summer of 1974. World central bankers had already turned toward monetary restraint, dooming hard assets such as copper and lumber to much lower prices. As we show in Chapter 8, commodity prices are affected early by swings in the monetary growth rates worldwide.

(4) That stocks were undervalued in the fall of 1974. Accelerating inflation and the general expectation that it would continue had knocked the market for a loop. But the workings of the money growth cycle indicated that a deceleration

of inflation was in hand at last. In Chapter 6 we show why stock prices respond positively to decelerating inflation. And respond they did, as the performance of the popular stock price averages in the first part of 1975 indicate.

History, of course, seldom repeats itself with precision. However, the same systematic responses of asset prices to the inflation cycle will persist into the future. And since the existence of the inflation cycle itself has become as certain as death and taxes, the successful investor must come to terms with the implications of high and volatile inflation for asset prices.

There are five principles that must be considered in building and maintaining an investment portfolio. Here is how they can be adapted to an investment environment characterized by high and volatile inflation.

DESIGN AN EFFICIENT PORTFOLIO

To take advantage of inflation's transfers, you must begin by thinking in terms of your total portfolio and balance sheet. Then you have to arrange them so that they efficiently serve the *Beat Inflation* goal.

Most of the hundreds of millions of dollars that have been spent on investment research over the years have been thrown down the drain. A major exception is the money that has been spent to develop the concept of an efficient portfolio. The real credit goes to two men who do not occupy plush offices and whose names are hardly household words: Harry Markowitz and William Sharpe.* According to Markowitz and Sharpe, an efficient portfolio is a collection of assets that maximize the return or income for a given level of risk. Therefore there are many efficient portfolios, depending

* See Harry M. Markowitz, "Portfolio Selection," *Journal of Finance,* March, 1952, and William F. Sharpe, "A Simplified Model for Portfolio Analysis," *Management Science,* January, 1963.

on the investor's goal and the amount of risk he is willing to accept.

The fact that you know the concept of an efficient portfolio is no guarantee of your investment results. All the MBA's running portfolios at those New York City banks also know the concept. But in professional money management it is only a little exaggeration to say that the goal of each portfolio manager has been to design the portfolio that is efficiently designed to be like that of every other portfolio manager. This has led to faddists' portfolios and their attendant problems. For obvious reasons, portfolio managers have a strong desire to play it safe in the sense of not doing much worse than anyone else. These problems show up most vividly in what has come to be known as a lack of liquidity in the stock market. When all professionals love Polaroid, they have a hard time finding anyone to be on the sell side, so its price shoots up beyond reason; when they all hate Polaroid they can't find anybody who will buy it, so it gets murdered.

Clearly you don't want a portfolio that is faddist, but one that is efficiently designed to meet the goal of beating inflation.

Once you get one of these portfolios in hand, you can afford to feel comfortable, but only for a while. Because, as inflation begins to push the price of your assets up, the faddists will start jumping in. At this point asset prices will begin to overdiscount inflation. It will be time to design a new portfolio to *Beat Inflation*. One will be available because you will be buying what the faddists are selling after the price drops.

DIVERSIFY

Not everybody who wants to beat inflation will buy the same portfolio. People have different tastes, preferences, likes and dislikes. They have different feelings on the amount of risk they are willing to accept. Here is where the old idea of diversification comes in. Although professional money managers have used this idea to justify portfolios that do not serve any goal efficiently, it does have some meaning to the *Beat Inflation* strategy.

During the course of designing your portfolio, you will decide that there is one investment at a given moment in time that is better than any other investment. But because the world is uncertain, there is some chance that you will be wrong. Therefore, the portion of your money that you will invest in that asset will depend on your attitude toward the possibility of losing everything. For even though you think the chances that your investment will turn sour are small, you feel you must hedge against that possibility; most people will want to diversify among several assets with *Beat Inflation* possibilities. Some of these will promise smaller returns but be safer than others.

Good diversification also means that the particular assets in your portfolio will complement each other. Suppose, again, that you start with the asset you like best, say cocoa commodity contracts whose chances of benefiting from inflation are grossly underestimated by the market. Suppose further that someone suddenly discovers that cocoa causes cancer in mice. Great as cocoa may be, like any single asset it carries with it some risks that you simply could not have foreseen. You are playing cocoa because you think it is cheap and cocoa stockpiles are low. You obviously wouldn't want all your assets in contracts that benefit from higher cocoa prices. Indeed, you would want some of them in assets that will benefit from inflation almost as much as cocoa contracts, but which can't be hurt by some bad news coming out about cocoa. Those investors who want to beat inflation can do it and still get some safety. This is what economists call minimizing the risk to obtain the highest possible return, and it is what Markowitz and Sharpe mean by efficient portfolios.

If you keep diversification and efficient portfolios in mind, you will not be suckered in by the Johnny One-Notes.

You don't get the safety of diversification by buying such close substitutes as gold, silver, platinum and diamonds. The efficient strategy for beating inflation requires that you not put all your eggs in one basket, or even in a number of extremely similar baskets.

In fact, one of the nice things about the *Beat Inflation* strategy is that it will ordinarily allow enormous diversification. A *Beat Inflation* portfolio could easily include say, some U.S. stocks, some Swiss time deposits, and maybe some forward marks (see Glossary). These days, a futures market for foreign exchange exists at the Chicago Mercantile Exchange. There, contracts are traded which allow the investor to speculate that the mark will rise in price.

TIME YOUR INVESTMENT DECISIONS CORRECTLY

The general investment-timing rule to beat inflation comes down to this: *Buy those assets whose prices do not fully reflect the benefits that inflation will bring. Sell those assets whose prices already overdiscount inflation.* There are special factors surrounding any particular asset, which means that inflation will have special effects on its price. However, the easy way to begin the exercise of judgment required to select the right vehicles is to compare the change that has occurred in its price to the change in the general price level over an appropriate period.

Take gold as an example. Figure 9 shows the relationship between the price of gold and the general price level as measured by the consumer price index. During most of the post-World War II period, gold was an extremely poor vehicle to beat inflation, as the chart illustrates, because its price even in the free market went up more slowly than prices in

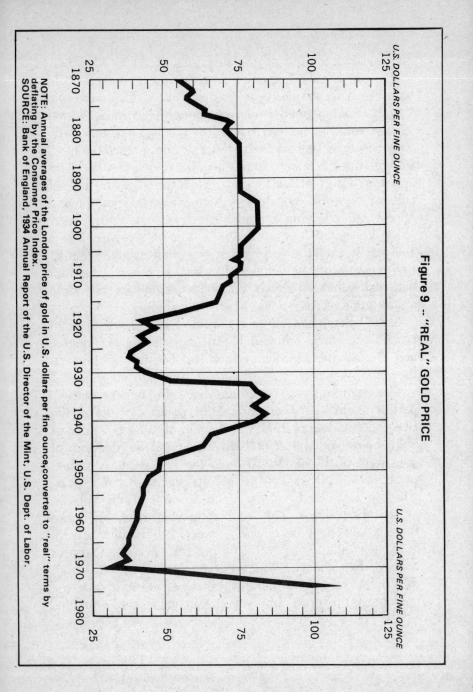

Figure 9 -- "REAL" GOLD PRICE

U.S. DOLLARS PER FINE OUNCE

U.S. DOLLARS PER FINE OUNCE

NOTE: Annual averages of the London price of gold in U.S. dollars per fine ounce,converted to "real" terms by
deflating by the Consumer Price Index.
SOURCE: Bank of England, 1934 Annual Report of the U.S. Director of the Mint, U.S. Dept. of Labor.

general. This should not be surprising. Gold is essentially useless and yields a negative return. That is to say, a gold bar or a certificate indicating you own one yields no interest. In fact, holding gold costs you money for insurance and storage and also interest payments if it was bought partly with borrowed money. So the price of gold limped along all through the 1950s and 1960s, since that period was not characterized by great fears over rapid inflation, while talk of collapse of world monetary systems was only sporadic and almost totally lacking in credibility.

By the year 1970, the price of gold had been carried to a 100-year low relative to prices in general. This kind of situation must always be watched by those who would beat inflation—because it always contains possibilities for rapid appreciation, if conditions change even slightly.

In 1971 they changed more than slightly. Governments all around the world adopted highly pro-inflationary policies, and the overvalued dollar, which had become the pivot of the world monetary system, began to tremble.

The environmental conditions for gold-buggery became perfect as inflation shot up and the dollar shot down. Between the middle of 1971 and the end of 1973, the price of gold almost tripled. In fact, between those dates, the price of gold went up by almost 20 times the rise in the consumer price index. Early in 1974 it shot up even higher to a point where it was clearly no longer cheap on a historical basis, as the chart shows. This kind of movement should make those who want to beat inflation wary. In fact, on April 15, 1974, when gold was at $173.50 per fine ounce, the authors advised their clients to sell gold and gold stocks. Although their lives were quite literally threatened by some extreme gold bugs, the price dropped 21 percent in three months.

Choose the Investment Whose Risk Level Lets You Sleep at Night

We have expressed a great deal of skepticism about the advice offered by the conventional money managers; but what they have been saying for years about the amount of risk that a person should be willing to take holds good in a world of perpetual and cyclical inflation. Generally, you should be willing to accept a high level of risk if you are young, have good income prospects from your job, and have considerable wealth. You should settle for lower-risk investments if you are old, have poor prospects of increasing your job income, and have little wealth.

Your psychological makeup also plays a role which often dominates. Some people are simply Nervous Nellies, no matter how young and rich they are, and they just can't sleep well if they are in high-risk investments. Others love to gamble, no matter how old and poor they may be. In short, when it comes to the risk level you are willing to accept, follow the advice of Socrates: "Know thyself."

We can tell you, however, that those willing to take the biggest risks are the ones who will stand to benefit from the most powerful of inflation transfers—that from net monetary creditors to net monetary debtors. As the accounting examples in Chapter 3 illustrated, it is by arranging your balance sheet properly that you can really make inflation work to your benefit in building up your net worth.

Choose the Right Currency in Which to Hold Your Assets

You should buy assets that are denominated in currencies of countries that will have the lowest inflation rates. Back when the fixed-exchange system prevailed, the exchange rate of a given country would stay constant for long periods of time even though the country was undergoing rapid domestic inflation compared to its trading partners. But when the currency values changed under this system, they changed by massive amounts.

Under the flexible-exchange-rate system that currently exists, however, you can be relatively certain that a country's exchange rate will quickly reflect its inflation prospects. Countries with low inflation rates will boost their exports relative to their imports. They experience trade surpluses. Countries with high inflation rates will boost their imports relative to their exports. They experience trade deficits.

The currencies of the trade-surplus nations tend to rise in value relative to the currencies of the trade-deficit nations. Therefore, to beat inflation, hold as much of your wealth as you can in countries that you expect to experience low inflation rates. But watch out. Make sure that the faddists haven't been there first. It could be true, for example, that Switzerland will experience a very low future inflation rate. But followers of some of the Johnny One-Notes who have been recommending Swiss francs may have driven the price of the Swiss franc way up—so high, in fact, that assets denominated in this currency are bad investments as compared to those denominated in other currencies that also have relatively good inflation outlooks.

There are in summary five conventional investment imperatives.

(1) Design an efficient portfolio.

(2) Diversify your portfolio.

(3) Time your buy and sell decisions correctly.

(4) Choose the risk level you feel comfortable with.

(5) Choose the right currency in which to denominate both your assets and your liabilities.

These are imperatives no matter what your investment goals may be. We have shown how they can be used to develop portfolios that will *Beat Inflation*. The portfolios will differ for different individuals. Each, however, will be based on the same premise: Assets will be bought whenever their prices do not reflect the benefits that inflation will bring. Assets will be sold as soon as they show signs of overanticipating the impact of the future inflation rate on their price.

5

How to Play
the *Beat Inflation* Game:
The Case of Bonds

The investor who beats inflation will always be holding the right combination of stocks, bonds, cash commodities and currencies. No one of these investment vehicles is for all seasons. But there is a season when each of them will be the right thing to hold to *Beat Inflation*.

The inflation trend will be high and the inflation cycle will be volatile. This means that nothing can be put away in your safe deposit box and forgotten, not even your jewelry. The *Beat Inflation* investor must be nimble, flexible, and always alert. Moreover, if he lets other people manage his money for him, he'd better be aware of what they are up to. If money managers are to *Beat Inflation* for you, they are going to have to adopt policies that will work within the context of a high trend rate of inflation and a volatile inflation cycle.

The right thing to do to *Beat Inflation* is to become an investor version of Pavlov's dog, who salivated every time the bell was rung. Successful investing in inflation requires certain automatic responses to signals of changes in the inflation rate.

Fortunately, these responses will not be hard to learn. As

you read the subsequent chapters of this book that deal with specific investment vehicles, you will discover that the response mechanism that will guide you in investing in stocks, bonds, cash, commodities, and currencies will always be the same. Therefore, the remainder of the book is a series of variations on three novel investment themes.

In this chapter we stick our toe in the investment waters by first stating these themes. We then apply them to the case of long-term bonds, that investment vehicle where the *Beat Inflation* strategy can be seen in its simplest and purest form. There are very few complications in the world of bonds. It provides the classic case of the *Beat Inflation* strategy in action.

To find the right portfolio for now—any particular moment in time—the investor must take three steps: (1) *Classify all investment vehicles by their appropriateness for accelerating and decelerating inflation.* Commodities, short-term cash-equivalent instruments such as commercial paper, large 90-day certificates of deposit or variable rate notes will benefit from accelerating inflation. Stocks and bonds will benefit from decelerating inflation. Currencies are a mixed bag and require a separate but related set of rules.

(2) *Decide whether inflation is about to accelerate or decelerate.* As we have seen, the basic rule here is to keep your eye on the money supply. Accelerations in the monetary growth rate lead to accelerations in the inflation rate. Sustained decelerations in the monetary growth rate lead to decelerations in the inflation rate.

(3) *See if the prices of particular assets incorporate your view of the inflation outlook.* Once you have decided whether inflation is about to accelerate or decelerate, see if the prices of stocks, bonds, commodities, short-term money-market instruments and currencies agree with your estimate. You know, for example, that stocks benefit from decelerating inflation. If you are in fact expecting inflation to decelerate

over the next six months, you will have one more decision to make before you conclude that stocks are the investment for the upcoming season. That decision will depend on whether the price of stocks *already reflects* a major deceleration in the inflation rate. If they don't, stocks are clearly right. If they do, there may be better alternatives available.

We are now ready to apply the *Beat Inflation* strategy to the case of bonds. Bonds are dull. But in certain circumstances they can be the perfect *Beat Inflation* vehicle. Certainly they provide the clearest example of how inflation creates and destroys wealth.

Unfortunately bondholders have had a lot more experience with the destruction of asset values than with their creation. Chances are that those investors who have bonds in their portfolios right now have observed at first hand how destructive inflation can be. Take a bunch of bonds issued by Ma Bell over the years. They are rated AAA by leading bond-rating services, meaning that they are viewed as carrying little or no risk of default. All bonds issued by Ma Bell came out at about $1,000 a bond—what people in the trade call par. In midsummer of 1974 one of these bonds, the 2⅝% of 1986—meaning the bonds pay out $26.25 in yield for each $1,000 face value—was selling for around $570 per bond. The 7% of 2001 were selling for about $780 per bond. The 8¾% of 2000 for about $940 per bond.

AT&T bonds are AAA, and the destruction in their value is minor compared to what happened to the bonds that are considered riskier because they are issued by companies that have a bigger chance of going bankrupt than Ma Bell. Here are some lurid mid-1974 examples for a few well-known companies. Pan American World Airways 4½% of 1986 were selling for $250 per bond, Eastern Airlines 5% of 1992 for $350 per bond, and TWA's 5% of 1994 at $340 per bond.

These companies didn't go out of business. They still pay

interest on their debt. They still provide services to the consumer. But the people who bought their IOUs are now really strapped. Even in the case of the AAA-rated company, the widows and orphans who bought AT&T 2⅝% at par were getting an interest rate of 2⅝% on their original investment at a time when inflation was in the double-digit range. To add to their psychological woes, all this was happening in a period when such AT&T subsidiaries as Pacific Telephone and Telegraph were coming out with bonds that were yielding over 9½% to new investors.

What happened? Certainly nobody tried to take advantage of anybody else; the companies didn't force investors to buy the 2⅝% bonds. In fact, it's almost certain the companies themselves didn't know what a bonanza they were getting when they originally marketed the bonds.

The reason that the bondholder was hurt and the bond issuer was helped was something that nobody foresaw. Inflation accelerated and the result was poison for bondholders in every imaginable way.

First of all, when inflation gets started, it begins the process of transferring income and wealth from the lender to the borrower. A bond is a commitment to pay a fixed number of dollars in interest per year—$26.25 in the case of the AT&T bonds mentioned above. When inflation starts to accelerate, the number of dollars in interest on newly issued bonds will be higher to compensate for the rise in the inflation rate; for example $95 per $1000 per year for the Pacific Tel, another issue mentioned above. When this happens, bonds already outstanding must fall in price to put their income stream in line with newly issued bonds. For example, the AT&T 2⅝% of 1986 must sell for $276.32 per $1000 par value for its yield to maturity to equal that of the newly issued 9½% Pacific Tel and Tel bonds. The 2⅝% lender is hurt in two ways. He is receiving less in terms of interest than he could on newly issued securities. Moreover, since the value of his security has fallen, he has suffered a decline in wealth. Thus there has been a transfer of both income and wealth from lender to borrower. Bonds were certainly the wrong play for the environment that was to come. Clearly they were a bad long-term holding.

In the old days, under the rules set up by the conventional investment advisers, bonds were an investment vehicle that you put at the bottom of your safe-deposit box; the coupons were to be clipped semiannually but the bonds were to be held until the redemption date. While not exciting, those rules were fine while prices were stable. But in the post-World War II years the trend rate of inflation was up—2 percent in the 1950s, 2.3 percent in the 1960s, and 6.1 percent in the 1970s. On a long-term basis, the widows and orphans who followed the conservative advice of the investment managers have been through an unending financial nightmare.

On average, bonds were a bad buy even if your investment horizon was relatively short. Periods in which the inflation rate accelerated lasted longer than periods in which the inflation rate decelerated. In each period of accelerating inflation interest rates on new bonds went up and the prices of existing bonds fell. Even in this dismal atmosphere there were periods when money could be made in bonds.

The common characteristic of all of these "good" periods was that inflation was decelerating. The last of these "good" periods was late 1974 and early 1975, when inflation decelerated and bond prices went up. A leveraged investor—one who borrowed on margin to buy bonds—could have made a bundle (and some did) during this period. But unfortunately, due to the way policy makers behave, these periods have been short and are likely to stay that way. For this reason, the whole approach to bond investing has to be changed.

Before inflation got started, the world of bonds was correctly geared to an economic environment in which the

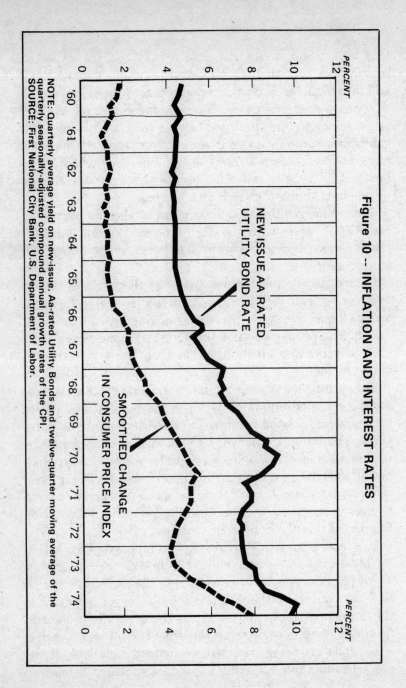

Figure 10 -- INFLATION AND INTEREST RATES

NEW ISSUE AA RATED
UTILITY BOND RATE

SMOOTHED CHANGE
IN CONSUMER PRICE INDEX

NOTE: Quarterly average yield on new-issue, Aa-rated Utility Bonds and twelve-quarter moving average of the quarterly seasonally-adjusted compound annual growth rates of the CPI.
SOURCE: First National City Bank, U.S. Department of Labor.

long-term inflation rate was close to zero and was expected to stay there. In that kind of world nothing mattered but whether the interest on that bond reflected the inherent risk of lending to a particular company. Indeed, bond analysts spent all their time in trying to figure out how fully the company's earnings covered the interest payments on various classes of bonds. It made a big difference whether the bondholder had the first claim on the assets of the company or whether he was further down the line.

These things still matter somewhat, as the comparison of the AT&T bonds with the Pan American World Airways bonds shows. But in a world of inflation, other things will matter more.

Figure 10, relating the movement of the inflation rate to bond prices and yields, shows that the big swing factor in today's bond market is the swing in the pace of price increase. The people who bought the AT&T bonds were suckered only because inflation, rather than being zero, turned out to be high.

Today, inflation dominates the bond market. Inflation rates are incorporated into bond yields in the simplest and purest way possible. A bond is normally issued for twenty or thirty years. The interest that will be paid each year is decided—in a marketplace where lenders and borrowers are continuously interacting—at the time the bond is issued. The interest rate carried at the time of issue incorporates borrowers' and lenders' expectations of what the inflation rate will be during the period that the bond is in existence.

The lender obviously wants to be compensated for giving up his purchasing power now. The interest rate does this. But if prices in general are expected to rise during the period that the bond is outstanding, he needs a bigger incentive in the form of higher interest rates. He demands protection from the adverse wealth transfer—from borrowers to lenders —that inflation brings. Indeed, economists now look at the market rate of interest, which in economic jargon is referred to as the "nominal" rate of interest, as the sum of two components—a "real" rate and an inflation premium.

The nominal rate is the rate that the market puts on newly issued bonds. And when you hear people talk about the current cost of long-term money, that is what they are talking about.

The real rate of interest is the rate that would prevail if prices were stable. Even if there were no inflation, lenders would demand compensation for giving up purchasing power now. Borrowers are willing to pay for credit because they figure they can use the money productively. In a world of stable prices the long-term interest rate is determined by the interaction of productivity and thrift. History suggests that the real rate of interest in the United States is approximately 3 percent.

The inflation premium is the extra compensation that lenders demand because they expect the dollars they give up today to buy less tomorrow. If prices are expected to rise at 2 percent per year, only the unsophisticated would be willing to lend without demanding an extra 2 percent in interest. For this reason an inflation premium over and above the return to productivity and thrift gets incorporated into interest rates during a period in which inflation is expected to exist.

Because the real rate of interest has been relatively constant over long periods of time, almost all the movement in long-term bond rates comes from changes in expectations about inflation—the inflation premium. Economic research also indicates that investors and borrowers tend to look at past rates of inflation when trying to guess at future rates of inflation. Figure 10 illustrates the relationship between the bond yield, in this case the rate on newly issued AA-rated utilities, and past rates of inflation as measured by the consumer price index. It shows that bond yields and past inflation rates are related.

Figure 10 shows that bond rates moved up when the inflation rate moved up and bond rates moved down when the inflation rate moved down.

Followers of the *Beat Inflation* strategy can make big money in bonds because there will be times when the inflation premium that is built into the market yields of bonds represents an incorrect estimate of the future inflation rate. Throw away the notion that bonds must be held to maturity. Only in a world of no inflation, or one in which the inflation rate is constant and fully reflected in the interest rate, does a buy-and-hold-to-maturity strategy make any kind of sense.

Bonds are pure debt; therefore the inflation-induced wealth transfer tends to occur quickly and with a vengeance in the bond market. The *Beat Inflation* investor can reap rich rewards from being on the right side of this transfer at the right time. Bonds, in a world where the inflation rate is likely to be variable, are anything but dull. U.S. Government bonds can be bought on margin with very little of your own money, and Uncle Sam's long-term IOUs can swing in price almost as much as Ma Bell's, even though there is less risk of default.

To make money by getting on the right side of the wealth transfer, the investor must follow several basic rules.

BOND RULE NO. 1

The right time to buy bonds is when the inflation rate incorporated into their yield exceeds your best judgment of the future rate of inflation. This is most likely to occur just before the inflation cycle moves into its decelerating phase.

This is the first investment rule stated in this book; there will be 35 others. With many rules, the decision as to whether to buy or sell turns on whether the market price or yield of the asset correctly incorporates the trend rate of inflation. Finding out what inflation rate is incorporated into the price of a particular asset can be complex. We are stating the bond rules before the stock rules, the commodity rules, and the currency rules because for bonds the rules are relatively simple.

The investor has two problems. First of all, he must determine the inflation rate built into the yield on newly issued long-term bonds. Second, he must determine what inflation rate ought to be built into the yield on long-term bonds, for once he does this he can easily form his best judgment yield on long-term securities.

The best judgment long-term bond yield is an important concept in the *Beat Inflation* strategy. It is by comparing the current market yield with the best judgment yield that the investor can decide whether long-term bonds are a buy or a sell.

Figure 11 shows you how to form your best judgment yield for long-term bonds. This yield is the yield that is consistent with your estimate of the trend rate of inflation. When yields on newly issued bonds rise above your best judgment yield you buy bonds; when yields on newly issued securities fall below your best judgment yield you sell bonds.

The best judgment rate is the simple sum of the real rate of interest plus the inflation premium that is consistent with the trend rate of growth of the money supply. The inflation premium that you use to get your best judgment interest rate reflects the trend rate of inflation implied by the monetary growth rate on a one-to-one basis. If the trend rate of inflation is 5 percent (money has been growing at 6 percent for the preceding two years), then the best judgment inflation premium is 5 percent; if money has been growing at 7 percent, the best judgment inflation premium is 6 percent, and so on.

To find out what inflation rate is being incorporated into current market bond yields, all that is required is to subtract about 3 percent from the current market yield on new issues. For example, if the stated interest rate on new bonds is 9 percent, it means that borrowers and lenders believe the inflation over the life of the bonds will average about 6 percent. To formulate your best judgment about the future inflation rate you must keep your eye on the money supply. If money

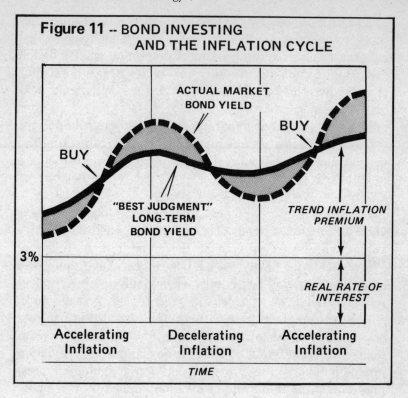

Figure 11 -- BOND INVESTING AND THE INFLATION CYCLE

ACTUAL MARKET BOND YIELD

BUY

BUY

"BEST JUDGMENT" LONG-TERM BOND YIELD

TREND INFLATION PREMIUM

3%

REAL RATE OF INTEREST

Accelerating Inflation   Decelerating Inflation   Accelerating Inflation

TIME

growth has been a steady 7 percent, the trend rate of inflation will be 6 percent. Therefore, in our example, bonds are a buy when yields rise over 9 percent; the higher the better for you.

To see how your ability to form a best judgment yield on long-term bonds would have made you money, compare the movement of the best judgment rate with that of the actual market long-term rate in Figure 11. The chart shows that the actual market yield exceeds the best judgment yield late in the accelerating phase of the inflation cycle and early in the decelerating phase. In fact, the difference is widest around the turning point in the inflation cycle. Therefore, the best

money-making opportunities occur just when the inflation
rate is about to decelerate. It is probably obvious to you, but
remember that when bond yields on newly issued bonds
fall, the prices on older bonds rise.

BOND RULE NO. 2

Move into lower quality or lower-rated bonds when you
believe the market is incorrectly reflecting the risk premium.
The biggest opportunities are likely to occur in lower-rated
bonds. Hairy as they may seem, plays on Ma Bell or U.S.
Government bonds are tame as compared to some lower-
rated bonds, such as those issued by the airlines. Ma Bell
always pays a lower rate of interest than Pan American
World Airways. The difference between the interest rate
paid by Ma Bell and Pan Am is an example of a risk premium. Just like the inflation cycle, there is a cycle in risk
premiums too. Most of the time the inflation cycle and the
risk-premium cycle move together. When inflation is accelerating, people will be talking about tight money and liquidity
crises, and the risk premium will be going up. The risk
premiums are likely to be the biggest in the final spasms of
accelerating inflation. Figure 12 schematically demonstrates
the widening and narrowing of the risk premium over the
inflation cycle.

Remember though, the lower you sink in the bond ratings,
the more risk you incur. Ordinarily, when you dip below
B-rated, the risk of default goes way up. The final spasm
of accelerating inflation is not hard to spot. When business
and economic news moves onto the front page of your newspaper, you are right smack in the middle of one. In the wake
of the Penn Central debacle in June of 1970, risk premiums
widened. They also widened when Con Edison omitted its
dividend and when Franklin National Bank went belly up.
For example, after Con Edison's board of directors announced their dividend omission on April 23, 1974, the

interest rate spread between AAA-rated corporate bonds and AA utilities widened from 87 basis points to 136 basis points in a matter of a few months. A basis point is one one-hundredth of a percentage point.

This fact has been documented with data going back to 1900. In a study, *Corporate Bond Quality and Investor Experience,* published by the National Bureau of Economic Research, W. Braddock Hickman found that when low-grade corporate bonds were purchased near the trough of an investment cycle (these correspond to peaks in our inflation cycle) the investor fared better than with similar purchases

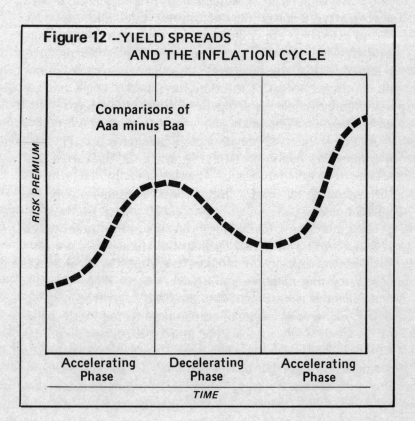

Figure 12 --YIELD SPREADS AND THE INFLATION CYCLE

Comparisons of Aaa minus Baa

RISK PREMIUM

Accelerating Phase   Decelerating Phase   Accelerating Phase

TIME

and sales of high-grade corporate bonds. He concluded that when low-grade bonds have been knocked way down in price, the market usually overestimates the risk of default. In fact, virtually all the economic research that has been done on the behavior of the risk premium shows that the risk premium has been more than enough to compensate the bondholder for additional risk. But be careful and remember the principle of diversification.

Penn Central bonds did default. But many other issues were tarnished by Penn Central, Con Edison and Franklin National Bank. It is in the nature of the securities markets to overdo things. After the Penn Central crisis evaporated, the risk premium narrowed again; the same was true after the Con Edison crisis and the Franklin National Bank crisis. For example, after Con Edison cut its dividend, the market in its typical knee-jerk fashion overreacted and risk premiums on *all* issues rose.

This overreaction represented a *Beat Inflation* opportunity. With inflation on the verge of decelerating risk premiums were bound to narrow. In fact, between July and November of 1974, the risk premium between AAA corporate bonds and AA utility bonds fell by 75 basis points. AA utility bonds normally yield more than AAA corporate bonds. This yield differential is generally regarded as a measure of the risk premium between the two rating classifications. When the dividend omission at Con Edison was announced, the risk premium widened. However, when investors had time to think about what happened, the risk premium began to fall. Consequently, the investor who bought AA utilities made an even greater killing than the one who played it safer.

BOND RULE NO. 3

The right time to incur long-term debt is when you expect the inflation rate to accelerate. It is the right time for the individual investor to become a net monetary debtor.

In a world of high and variable inflation the correct time to take on debt is during those brief periods when interest rates fall. These periods will occur during the decelerating phase of the inflation cycle. And the bottom in interest rates is likely to occur toward the end of the decelerating phase and just prior to reacceleration.

This is an extremely critical period for the *Beat Inflation* investor. The strategy will require him to rearrange his portfolio. One step that he certainly ought to take is to increase the degree to which he is a net monetary debtor. This means that he should increase his holdings of real assets (commodities, real estate) and finance his buying spree with the profits that he is likely to have made in the stock market and, most importantly, with long-term debt.

How you go about increasing your long-term debt depends on who you are and how rich you are. No matter what your position, though, you should start thinking like the big corporate treasurer and see what avenues are really open to you so that you can borrow money at favorable rates that will be available just prior to the upswing in the inflation cycle. When you do this you will find a surprising number of options available.

The key is to try to borrow at fixed rates which will be relatively low at the bottom of the inflation cycle. One possibility, if you have not already done it, would be to borrow the cash value of your life insurance. Also possible, but much more risky, is to arrange a second mortgage on your home and put the money to work in real estate or commodities. Don't forget your friendly neighborhood banker. Banks are apt to be flush with money toward the end of the decelerating phase of the inflation cycle. And most investors simply do not exploit the possibilities of using personal credit from their banks. Never be afraid of your banker—remember he makes his money by lending to you, not by accepting your deposits.

BOND RULE NO. 4

When the *Beat Inflation* strategy tells you bonds are a buy, you can maximize your profits at no additional risk by buying a portfolio of discount bonds. A discount bond in a world where a high trend rate of inflation has pushed the trend of interest rates upward, is simply a bond that was issued some time in the past. For example, the Ma Bell 2⅝% of 1986 are deep discount bonds. They are selling way below their par value because their coupon interest rate is far below the coupon on newly issued bonds. Studies by Salomon Brothers indicate that during bull markets in bonds, discount bonds give the investor a higher total return than a similar amount of newly issued bonds. During the bond bull market in the third quarter of 1970, for example, the total return to holding discount bonds was 36 percent at an annual rate compared to only 25 percent for newly issued bonds. Similarly, when bond prices are falling a portfolio of discount bonds performs worse than a portfolio of newly issued bonds or premium bonds.

BOND RULE NO. 5

Those investors who want to play the interest-rate swings to the hilt ought to take advantage of the rotation in the yield curve. The yield curve is a shorthand expression that bond-market people use to describe the relationship between interest rates on short maturity and longer maturity debt instruments. A positively sloped yield curve exists when short rates are lower than long rates. Figure 13 shows the positively sloped yield curve that existed in the spring of 1971. A negatively sloped yield curve exists when short-term rates are higher than long-term rates. Figure 14 shows the negatively sloped yield curve that existed in July 1974. In the pre-inflation-cycle days, the yield curve had a positive slope most of the time. But now that high and variable inflation is

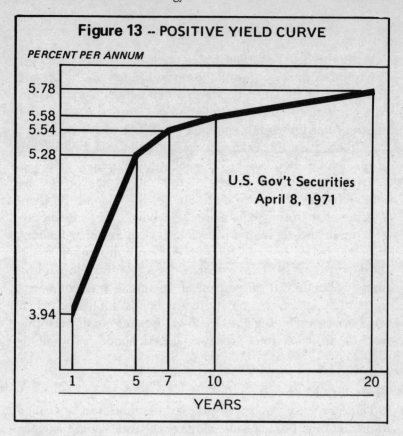

Figure 13 -- POSITIVE YIELD CURVE

PERCENT PER ANNUM

U.S. Gov't Securities
April 8, 1971

YEARS

here to stay, the yield curve will show wide and relatively frequent fluctuations. Short-term rates will be higher than long-term rates toward the peak in the inflation cycle; short-term rates will be lower than long-term rates toward the bottom of the inflation cycle. This means that short-term rates swing more than long-term rates over the inflation cycle, and herein lies an opportunity for financing your investments in a most profitable way.

Why does the yield curve swing from positively sloped to negatively sloped? Tomes have been written on this by a

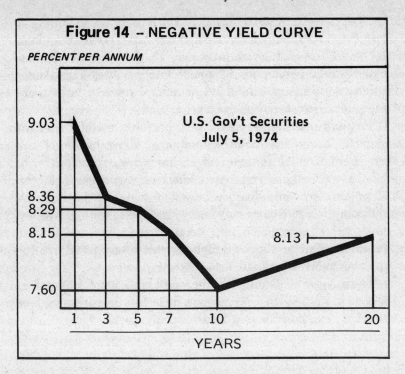

Figure 14 -- NEGATIVE YIELD CURVE

PERCENT PER ANNUM

U.S. Gov't Securities
July 5, 1974

9.03

8.36
8.29
8.15
8.13

7.60

1   3   5   7   10   20

YEARS

number of authors, including some of the great names in economics such as John Maynard Keynes. While all the explanations differ to some degree, they all incorporate a similar idea. When interest rates are extremely high by historic standards, investors expect them to come down. They are therefore willing to lend for long periods of time at lower rates. When rates are low by historic standards, investors expect them to rise. They therefore demand a higher interest rate for long-term money than for short-term money and borrowers with similar views of the outlook are willing to pay it.

The yield curve will be steeper for a negatively sloped yield curve if everybody is looking for a big decline in interest rates over the near term. When it is upward-sloping it will be steeper in an upward direction if everybody is looking for a big rise in interest rates over the near future. If your expectation of inflation and hence interest rates is markedly different from that embodied in market interest rates there may be a *Beat Inflation* play.

For example, if the yield curve has only a slight upward slope to it and you believe inflation is about to surge, and hence interest rates will move dramatically upward, you would do well to keep your financial investments in the short-term area and do what borrowing you can in the long-term market. This is because long-term interest rates will not incorporate a large enough inflation premium to warrant purchase. You would get a higher return by constantly turning over short-term financial assets.

Similarly you should borrow short and lend long when the yield curve is not steep enough in the downward direction and inflation is about to decelerate sharply.

6

Inflation and Common Stocks

Ten years ago a book on how to beat inflation would have been published, written and paid for by Merrill Lynch, Pierce Fenner and Smith. They wouldn't have had 29 ways to be bullish on America. They would have had one primary way: Buy common stocks. And although almost everyone who took that advice has seen his portfolio go up in smoke, Merrill Lynch wouldn't have been wrong. In the 1950s and most of the 1960s, stocks were a super investment vehicle, outperforming everything else.

This was so even though stocks were being sold on what proved to be a false premise. Merrill Lynch and everyone else who was then selling stocks kept advertising equities as the ideal hedge against inflation. The investor was told that equity investment—a share of ownership—was the only way to keep ahead of rising prices. The only alternative that investment advisers and brokers thought was suitable for the prudent man—bonds—yielded only a fixed number of dollars per year. Stocks, by contrast, could be expected to provide an ever-growing stream of dividends, which in the case of growth stocks was assumed to grow to the sky, but this wouldn't happen until way in the future.

The 1950s and the first half of the 1960s was a period when everybody turned to Wall Street for protection against inflation. And, in fact, the day in 1958 that the American Telephone and Telegraph Company decided to invest their employees' pension money in common stocks rather than just in the traditional bonds, what Murray Rossant, now director of the Twentieth Century Fund, called "the cult of equities" was born. The American Telephone and Telegraph pension-fund managers were the Episcopal bishops of this cult. Its Holy Rollers were the go-go fund managers of the late 1960s who bid up the prices of the stocks of untried companies. Where are the conglomerates now? Where are the men whose names were magic in the brokers' boardrooms? Like the go-go funds they are gone-gone.

The cult of equities is dead now, killed by the very thing that was supposed to be giving it life—inflation. As long as inflation remained only a sales argument, it could be used to justify the cult of equities, and stocks sold well. But, ironically, when inflation actually began in earnest, it played hob with the fundamental determinants of stock prices.

The reason inflation has undermined the stock market is essentially simple. It can be found in *Security Analysis,* a book written in 1934 by two professors at the Columbia University Business School, Benjamin Graham and David L. Dodd. The book is the security analysts' bible.

It suggests a simple equation that accurately portrays the fundamental determinants of the value of a stock. The equation has three elements: expected profits and dividend growth, expected interest rates, and some measure of risk. When expected profits go up, stock prices go up; when expected interest rates go down, stock prices go up; when investors feel more certain about future profits and interest rates, stock prices go up. When inflation actually came, it dumped the market. Inflation fouled up corporate earnings; inflation jacked up interest rates; inflation made people far more uncertain about the outlook for interest rates and profits.

Inflation makes real profits hard to come by, hard to understand and therefore hard to trust. From 1966 to the bottom of the 1970 recession, corporations were on the wrong side of inflation-induced income transfers. Inflation was concentrated in wages, services, construction and borrowing charges. This meant that the costs of staying in business went up and profits were small. Profits actually declined, even though prices went up. So instead of being a hedge against inflation, stocks bore the brunt of inflation. After-tax profits fell by 26.3 percent in current dollars over the period. Adjusted for inflation they fell even more—39.9 percent. In the battle for who gets what out of the economic pie, the profits share of Gross National Product plummeted, while the wage and salary share rose.

Beginning in late 1970 things started to look up for profits. Wages had more than caught up with past inflation, and inflation itself began to decelerate and brought interest rates down with it. In 1970, the inflation rate was running 5.9 percent; in 1971, 4.3 percent; in 1972, 3.3 percent. At the same time that the inflation rate was coming down, corporate profits started up, pulling stock prices with them. Hence, as the economy moved from a more inflationary environment to a less inflationary environment, profits did better, stocks did better and the old saw that stocks were a hedge against inflation was turned on its head.

The irony became total in 1973 and 1974. Inflation really heated into the double-digit range, and this time profits really responded. Commodity prices led the advance, and wholesale prices rose much faster than wages. But, even though profits were rising, stocks got creamed. Again the accelerating phase of the inflation cycle killed the market. This time the problem wasn't sluggish profits; it was that nobody trusted the profits numbers.

Rising prices create two big problems in the arithmetic of profits reporting. Both problems make the profits numbers larger than they should be, and larger than they can be expected to be if the inflation rate slows down.

One problem is the big gains that companies make on the products and materials that they already have on hand when inflation accelerates. These gains are reported in the profits figures and are taxed. But people know that any ongoing business has to replace the stock in its inventory. The profits generated by inventories can't be used in any other way. They are not available to pay stockholders dividends or to buy new plants and equipment or to pay for the research needed to develop new products. Therefore, profits coming from inventory windfalls are not the basis to build stock market dreams on. In the realistic world of 1973 and 1974, the average investor recognized this.

Depreciation raises a second problem that is even more obvious. As part of the cost of doing business, companies charge off the cost of replacing their equipment, so that when it wears out they will have funds available to replace it. The guidelines for how big these expenses can be are laid out by the Internal Revenue Service—hence, the bigger they are, the slimmer corporate tax collections will be. When prices rise, so does the cost of replacing equipment. It's universally accepted that inflation renders depreciation charges inadequate to replace the equipment. As a consequence, profits are overstated. And, to add insult to injury, these overstated profits are taxed.

Inflation also pumps up interest rates, making other financial assets relatively attractive as compared to common stocks. When interest rates go sky high, as they did in 1973-1974, stock prices hit the skids.

Inflation increases uncertainty, raising doubts about the future profitability of American industry. When inflation strikes, people have more legitimate reasons to worry than when prices are stable. Inflation brings with it three big worries:

Fear of recession. Although government policy has become far more permissive on inflation then it used to be, rampant price increases will meet with some response from Washington—a throttling back of the rate of monetary expansion. This in turn leads to recession, dumping corporate profits and increasing business failures.

Fear of financial collapse. Inflation brings sky-high interest rates. And since interest rates and financial asset prices move in different directions, this could spell trouble for banks, other financial institutions and even ordinary companies. These institutions are on the wrong side of the wealth transfer. They are stocked with lots of IOUs that they can't sell for their face value. When interest rates shoot up, any bank that has to liquidate will be insolvent. This is what happened to the Franklin National Bank in early 1974. The market value of the Franklin's liabilities exceeded the market value of its assets.

Fear of worldwide depression. Countries are much more interdependent than they used to be so liquidity crises in one country can spill over to other countries. Many strange new international financial markets, such as the Eurodollar market, have come into being. Together with the system of floating exchange rates, these markets increase the risk inherent in financial transactions, particularly for banks and other financial institutions. When rapid inflation brings sharply escalating interest rates around the world, worries over a world financial crisis intensify.

Ira U. Cobleigh once wrote a book entitled *Happiness Is a Stock That Doubles in a Year.* No stock will double *every* year in an inflationary period. But the investor who obeys the following six rules can and will find stocks that have the potential of doubling at some points in the inflation cycle.

STOCK MARKET RULE No. 1

Buy stocks when your best judgment of the future rate of inflation is markedly less than the rate of inflation that the public expects. Sell stocks (or sell them short) when the trend rate of inflation that the public (and the stock market) expects is less than your best judgment rate.

As in the case of bonds, the investor needs to know two things in order to make stock market decisions. First of all, he must establish his own best estimate of the future inflation rate and the implication of this inflation rate for stock prices. Second, he must determine the future inflation rate that is built into current stock prices. Your buy and sell decisions are importantly, but not solely, based on a comparison of your best judgment of the inflation rate with the future inflation rate that is built into current stock prices.

In Chapter 2 we explained how you should determine your own best judgment estimate of the future inflation rate. Here, we will show you how to calculate the inflation rate that is built into current stock prices as well as how you can use your best judgment inflation rate to obtain an estimate of where the stock market ought to be and therefore is likely to move.

Calculating the inflation rate that is built into stock prices requires a small dose of mathematics. But we believe that the time invested in grasping the simple equation and using it will pay off handsomely. Enormous amounts of money have been lost in the stock market since 1965, primarily because of a failure to recognize how the inflation cycle impacts stock prices.

The equation we use is a variant of the Graham and Dodd equation. It says $P = D/(k-g)$. In the equation

$P =$ stock prices; in our example we will use the Dow Jones Industrial Average.

D = current dividends; in our example we will use a measure of the current dividends on the thirty stocks in
the Dow Jones average.

k = the expected rate of return. That means it is the total
return that investors expect to get from investing in
stocks at current prices.

g = the expected rate of growth in dividends. This simply
is the rate at which investors believe dividends will
grow in the future.

This equation allows you to determine what inflation rate
is built into stock prices. To illustrate this, let's see what the
equation would have shown at the end of 1974. P, or the
Dow Jones average, was around 600. D, or dividends on the
Dow Jones stocks, were $38. You can't determine what k and
g are by looking at the financial pages.

In order to determine what values to use for g and k you
must make some assumptions. To estimate g, simply take the
trend rate of inflation and add 3 percent to it. The 3 percent
figure is our estimate of the real growth dividends. The trend
rate of inflation is an old friend. At the end of 1974, it was 5
percent, the trend rate of inflation consistent with a money-
supply growth rate of 6 percent.

In our formulation of a *Beat Inflation* strategy for stocks, k
swings with the inflation cycle. Stocks are alternatives to
other investments. In order to buy stocks an investor must
be persuaded that his purchase will pay off as well as an
investment in short-term liquid assets, long-term bonds, and
commodities. Because the return from other assets, such as
short-term liquid assets and commodities, moves up during
the accelerating phase of the inflation cycle, so must k. Similarly, when rates of return on alternative investments fall in
the decelerating phase of the cycle, so does k.

The key to stock investing is to remember that whatever
pushes k up is bad for stocks and whatever pushes it down
is good for stocks. When k goes up, the market applies a

higher rate of discount to the current level of dividends, and thus P (stock prices) falls.

Like bond yields, k is composed of a real rate component and an inflation premium. And since the real rate doesn't vary much over time, the movements up and down in k occur because of changes in inflation expectations in the stock market.

We are now ready to figure out whether stocks are a buy or a sell at various stages of the inflation cycle and various levels of the stock market. Our basic example is drawn from the situation that prevailed at the end of 1974 when the Dow Jones Industrial stocks were paying $38 in dividends and the market was around 600. Remembering that we estimate g to be 8 percent, based on previous trends in the monetary growth rate, solving the equation for k shows that the expected rate of return was 14.3 percent at the end of 1974. The question for the *Beat Inflation* investor is what estimate of the inflation rate does this expected rate of return contain. The Klein-Wolman answer is 8.3 percent because our research indicates that the real rate of return to stocks in a world that has adjusted to the inflation cycle is around 6 percent. Therefore, at the end of 1974, 8.3 percent was the inflation rate built into stock prices.

The *Beat Inflation* investor should have compared this to his own best judgment estimate of the future inflation rate. At the end of 1974 the economy was in the initial stages of decelerating inflation and the Klein-Wolman estimate of the trend rate of inflation was 5 percent. Plugging a 5 percent inflation premium into k gives you a value for k of 11 percent. And solving the equation this time for P gives you your best judgment value for the Dow Jones for 5 percent inflation— a value of 1266 for the Dow Jones. Clearly the market was a buy at the end of 1974; our formula indicated that stock prices could double as inflation expectations were receding during the decelerating phase of the inflation cycle. Figure

15 solves the equation for various inflation premiums using the $38 dividend figure for 1974. The figure illustrates how dramatically stock prices respond to changes in the inflation premium. This exercise also tells you how well a bet on stocks is covered. For example, if the trend rate of inflation turns out to be 7 percent instead of 5 percent, stock prices should be 26.6 percent higher than they were at the end of 1974.

This arithmetic is a basic part of your tool kit, but don't get carried away with it. The calculations are based on trend rates of inflation and take no account of the way the inflation cycle influences expectations in the stock market. When inflation is accelerating, the stock market is apt to be far more nervous than when it is decelerating. And although the equation may indicate that stocks are a buy, remember all of the problems that accelerating inflation raises for stock prices and corporate profits. Therefore, the equation should only lead you to buying decisions when the economy is in the decelerating phase of the inflation cycle.

FIGURE 15

THE INFLATION PREMIUM AND STOCK PRICES

Inflation Premium in Stock Prices	Value of Dow Index
4%	1,900
5%	1,266
6%	950
7%	760
8%	633
9%	542
10%	475

Note: Stock prices calculated by assuming g=8 percent, the real component of k=6 percent, and D=$38.

Unless inflation is decelerating or about to decelerate, you don't want stocks—any stocks. Get rid of them—really get rid of them. When money managers tell *Wall Street Journal* reporters that they are in cash, they generally mean that they have changed their portfolios from 10 percent cash and 90 percent stocks to 15 percent cash and 85 percent stocks. Do not emulate them. When you expect inflation to be worse than the market expects it to be, get out of stocks. Under these circumstances there will be other good places to be: commodities—including gold—and short-term money instruments.

By the same token, when you expect the rate of inflation to be materially less than the market expects, stocks will be an ideal vehicle; so will some bonds.

STOCK MARKET RULE NO. 2

The richest stock market rewards will occur just before the inflation rate begins to decline. A declining inflation rate will change the elements in Graham and Dodd's equation in such a way as to jack up equity values on a fundamental basis. Stocks become a good play when the inflation cycle is in the declining phase. For a fleeting moment stocks will regain the glow that made them stars in the 1950s and early 1960s.

The ideal time to be in stocks is just before the decline in inflation occurs, and certainly before the fact that it is occurring becomes widely recognized. The *Beat Inflation* strategist will have advance warning of the impending turnaround in the inflation rate because he will have been tracking the money supply. Moreover, commodity prices already will have weakened, and short-term interest rates will be above long-term interest rates. Everyone will be pessimistic; there will be more bearish recommendations about stocks than bullish recommendations; fund managers will be telling *The*

Wall Street Journal that they are moving into cash. In short, conditions will be ideal to buy.

STOCK MARKET RULE NO. 3

When the stock market looks good, put your money on the high *beta* horses. *Beta* is more than the second letter in the Greek alphabet. It is the symbol that statisticians and econometricians use to measure the volatility of a given stock relative to the overall stock market. Suppose that an econometrician calculates the *beta* for the XYZ Corporation to be 1.5. This means that in the past the price of this stock has on the average increased 50 percent more than stocks in general when the market was rising, and decreased 50 percent faster than stocks in general when the market was falling. In short, XYZ Corporation is a high *beta* stock—one that is more volatile than stocks in general. A stock with a *beta* of 1.0 would on the average be about as volatile as stocks in general, while stocks with a *beta* of less than 1.0 would be on the average less volatile than most stocks.

When he expects the stock market to go up, an investor who is willing to take some risk will do much better than the market if he constructs his portfolio by buying stocks with *betas* significantly greater than 1.0.

A simple way to do this is to buy a no-load mutual fund whose *beta* is significantly greater than 1.0. You have to pay a sales commission of up to 8½ percent on most mutual funds, particularly those that are sold by brokers. This means that for every $100 you put in you only have $91.50 working for you when you start. With a no-load there is no sales charge, so $100 out of every $100 put in is at work and it doesn't have to rise by 8.5 percent just to get even. Moreover, the evidence indicates that no-load funds perform just as well and just as badly as funds that charge sales commissions. Figure 16 shows the *betas* for 25 well-known stocks. Figure 17 shows the *betas* for 25 seasoned no-load funds.

FIGURE 16

BETAS FOR 25 WELL-KNOWN STOCKS

Company	Beta
American Telephone & Telegraph	.75
Avon Products	1.20
Black & Decker Manufacturing	1.20
Burroughs Corp.	1.40
Citicorp	1.25
Eastman Kodak	1.05
Eli Lilly & Co.	1.00
Emerson Electric Co.	1.00
Exxon Corp.	.95
General Reinsurance Corp.	1.00
Halliburton Co.	1.10
Imperial Oil Ltd.	.85
International Business Machines	1.05
Merck & Co.	1.05
Mobil Oil	.95
Pepsico Inc.	1.05
Polaroid	1.45
Schlumberger Ltd.	1.10
Sears Roebuck & Co.	1.00
Sony Corp. ADR	1.05
Standard Oil of California	1.05
Syntex Co.	1.30
Walt Disney Productions	1.40
Weyerhaeuser & Co.	1.05
Xerox Corp.	1.20

Source: Value Line Investment Service.

FIGURE 17

BETAS FOR 25 SELECTED NO LOAD FUNDS

Fund	Objective	Beta
Afuture Fund	Maximum Capital Gains	1.55
American Investors	Maximum Capital Gains	1.26
Babson	Growth	1.06
Beacon Hill	Growth	0.92
Colonial Growth Shares	Growth	1.11
Columbia Growth	Maximum Capital Gains	1.06
Dodge & Cox Stock Fund	Growth and Current Income	0.98
Drexel Equity	Growth	0.95
Edie Special Growth	Maximum Capital Gains	1.16
Energy Fund	Growth	0.92
Foursquare Fund	Growth	1.13
Growth Industry Shares	Growth	1.11
Guardian Mutual Fund	Growth, Income & Stability	0.96
Johnston Mutual Fund	Growth	1.08
Mathers Fund	Maximum Capital Gains	1.07
National Industries Fund	Growth, Income & Stability	1.08
Neuwirth Fund	Maximum Capital Gains	1.12
Nicholas Fund	Maximum Capital Gains	1.54
Northeast Investors Trust	Income	0.23
One William Street	Growth and Current Income	1.05
Price Growth Fund	Growth	1.17
Rowe Price New Era	Growth	0.89
Rowe Price New Horizons	Maximum Capital Gains	1.24
Scudder International Investment	Growth	0.60
Selected American Shares	Growth and Current Income	0.97

Source: Wiesenberger Services, Inc.

The *Beat Inflation* investor, however, need not always use high *betas* for leverage. A portfolio with a *beta* of 1.0 (say the 30 stocks in the Dow Jones Industrial Average) bought on margin will ordinarily serve you just as well as a high-*beta* portfolio. If you buy stocks that do no better than the market as a whole with 50 percent borrowed money, you will do just as well as if you bought a portfolio of stocks whose average *beta* was 1.5.

STOCK MARKET RULE NO. 4

Be sure you know the impact that inflation is having on the companies whose stocks you are planning to buy. Remember that inflation distorts income statements and balance sheets. Accelerating inflation gives a false glow to corporate profits because it leads to large inventory profits and inadequate depreciation reserves. When Arab oil ministers started to apply the economics they had learned at the Harvard Business School and quadrupled oil prices, oil companies benefited because their oil inventories immediately became much more valuable. They reported enormous profits gains in late 1973 and early 1974, but their stockholders saw little benefit. The value of their shares basically went nowhere.

One reason was the fear that the government would grab a big share of the windfall profits. Another was the recognition that the surge in profits was temporary and would dwindle once the oil companies used up their lower-priced oil inventories. In a sense this is a classic example of inflation's effect on reported profits and why profits attributed to inflation should be examined carefully.

The steel industry contains many companies that reported excellent profits during the inflationary surge in late 1973 and 1974. Inventory profits were important here too, but the inadequacy of depreciation allowances also played a critical role. These companies' stock prices did not respond to higher profits in the usual way. The inventory profits in the steel industry were heavily discounted, as they were in the oil industry. But recognition that depreciation allowances would be inadequate to replace worn-out equipment created skepticism that the high profits could be maintained without massive additional financing. This shows up most clearly in the difference between the book value—the value assigned to the company by the accountants on the basis of the historical or purchase price of its net assets—and its market value. For most steel companies this gap was very large. For example, Wheeling Steel had a book value of $79.38 per share on December 31, 1973, and on the same day its market price was $13. Jones and Laughlin was worth $44.99 per share, according to the accountants, but the stock was selling for $18.88.

A big difference between book value and market value has never been a good reason to buy stock. This is particularly true when inflation is high and volatile.

STOCK MARKET RULE No. 5

Seek opportunities in interest-rate sensitive stocks when inflation begins to decelerate.

All stocks tend to move in the opposite direction from the interest rate. But some stocks respond particularly to changes in short-term interest rates—rates on treasury bills, commercial paper and bank certificates of deposit. Among the stocks most sensitive to interest rates are those of finance companies, real estate investment trusts, and savings and loan associations. In general these companies borrow short term and lend longer term. Short-term rates move up and down with changes in the inflation rates more quickly than long-term rates. Hence, when inflation decelerates, short-term rates come down more than long-term rates, and the profits of these companies rise. When inflation accelerates, just the opposite happens.

STOCK MARKET RULE NO. 6

Recognize that most companies deal in a world market. And, in a world of volatile and permanent inflation, recognize that those companies with major exposure in countries with relatively low inflation rates will do best. Here is one point where we have to get ahead of ourselves. Chapter 9 will show that profits can be made from holding the currencies of countries with the lowest trend rates of inflation. Because the value of their currencies will rise, profits earned in these countries will become higher when valued in terms of dollars.

These six rules will allow you to use stocks to *Beat Inflation*. They say that stocks are the best bets when inflation is decelerating and poor bets when it's accelerating. Like bonds, stocks should never be put in your safe-deposit box and forgotten. The *Beat Inflation* investment race will be won by the nimble.

7

Cash: How Much Should You Keep and Where Should You Keep It

In a world of high inflation, how you manage your cash, that ready-access portion of wealth that people used to unthinkingly keep in their pockets, or checking account or savings account when inflation did not matter, is extremely important. When interest rates are sky high, cash management can make a major difference in how well you *Beat Inflation*.

A few years ago, investment advisers had no need to write a chapter about cash management. The reason was simple: People advised against storing money under the mattress but the advice ended there. In general, the rules to follow came right out of Poor Richard: Keep enough in your checking account for monthly expenses, plus a little for emergencies, and what's left over keep in a savings account.

Everybody, including the tight-fisted treasurer of a giant corporation, followed these rules until the early 1960s. But then some of the nation's corporations, helped by some of the nation's giant banks, began to play an exciting new game called "intensive cash management." Those who want to *Beat Inflation* would do well to learn some of the rules for playing this game. What is good for General Motors is good for you, too. And the financial world is changing in a way that allows the individual investor some of the cash plays that were available only to the giant corporations a few years ago.

The new routes available for intensive cash management will sometimes play a critical role in the *Beat Inflation* strategy. There will be times when you will want most of your investable funds in them. For example, between the beginning of April and the end of September in 1974, short-term money market instruments, such as U.S. Government treasury bills and prime commercial paper, were the only place to be. For, while everything else from gold to soybeans to Polaroid was on the skids, yields on short-term money market instruments zoomed. So the smart investor could earn 12 percent or more with little risk in money market instruments and wait for other *Beat Inflation* opportunities to arise.

High inflation and high interest rates have meant a growing public awareness that it is easy to put out money for extremely short periods of time at high rates. Banks, for example, lend money to each other quite literally overnight for use during one working day in the Federal Funds market. Almost the same option is available to the smaller investor in the new money market funds that are being announced each day. So there is no reason not to lend your money out at high rates, even if you know you are going to need it soon—perhaps tomorrow.

The game of intensive cash management is safe and simple. The treasurer of the giant corporation follows certain simple rules in playing it. To beat inflation you should follow them too.

CASH MANAGEMENT RULE No. 1

Keep that portion of your portfolio which yields zero interest at a minimum. When asked how much noninterest-bearing cash they think it advisable to hold, some corporate treasurers answer "None." Their reasoning is straightforward. As long as they can see at least some interest on their money elsewhere, they ought to keep no cash. Theoretically, the correct amount of currency to keep in cash and in checking accounts is zero.

This should be your goal, but it is an ideal goal no one can attain. Just think what an inconvenient life you would lead if you really did this. Every payday you could deposit your paycheck in a day of deposit–day of withdrawal savings account and receive the maximum interest rate the law allows, which may be far less than the market interest rate. Every time you needed money you would stand in line at your savings bank and submit your withdrawal slip. If at the end of the month you added up the number of hours you spent with your favorite teller and in line, you would find that the interest credited to your account would compensate you at the rate of only a few pennies per hour. You probably have better things to do with your time. The difference between you and the corporate treasurer, of course, is that he is dealing with millions, and thus the interest return is worth somebody's time.

Although it is impossible, or at least impractical, to try to emulate the corporate treasurer, the individual investor could probably get by with less cash if he put some effort into it.

Cash Management Rule No. 2

Keep no excess funds in your checking account. There is no reason to keep emergency funds there. Bad as it may be as a *Beat Inflation* play, a day of deposit–day of withdrawal account in a savings bank is a better place for emergency funds. If you are afraid of running your checking account down too low and having a check bounce, get an overdraft privilege. In days when interest rates are sky high, as in mid-1974, the overdraft privilege can be a cheap source of funds. Take advantage of the government pressure on banks to keep the rates of interest on consumer borrowing low. In mid-1974, rates on consumer overdraft loans were the same as the prime rate—the rate that the banks charge their best corporate customers. When the *Beat Inflation* strategy suggests that the time to move is now, don't hesitate to leverage your bank for every cent you can get out of it. The *Beat Inflation* strategy frequently turns up investment opportunities with high reward-risk ratios when interest rates are very high and money is hard to come by. To make sure that he can get his hands on plenty of money in periods like this, a corporate treasurer arranges for lines of credit well in advance. He does not have access to these funds for nothing. There is a charge to a corporation for a guaranteed line of credit. The individual investor can get the same privilege for nothing. Get it! Remember: Banks are institutions that are famous for handing out snow in the winter and umbrellas when the sun is shining.

Remember also Ogden Nash's admonition to would-be bankers:

> One rule which woe betides the banker
> who fails to heed it:
> Never lend money to anybody
> unless they don't need it.

The right time to arrange for your line of credit is not when credit is scarce but when there is plenty of it around. You will be able to get a bigger credit line if you tap your bank when credit is plentiful. And banks are honorable; once they give you a credit line, they rarely take it away.

CASH MANAGEMENT RULE NO. 3

Obtain the highest return possible consistent with safety for your funds. Not too many years ago the individual investor had few choices. He could put funds in currency, in a checking account, or a savings account. Even the day of deposit–day of withdrawal account is relatively new. Previously the individual investor forfeited interest on a savings account if the money was withdrawn prior to the end of a quarter. But, consider the rich variety of alternative places to put cash you have available now:

• Savings banks are offering a choice of maturities as well as the day of withdrawal–day of deposit account. We consider funds placed for ninety days or less liquid enough to serve as an emergency fund or as a haven for investment funds when other alternatives don't offer *Beat Inflation* opportunities. Savings deposits are riskless—they are FDIC insured up to $40,000 per account.

• Money market instruments are offered for sale by the U.S. Treasury, and by large and very creditworthy corporations and banks. The safest of these instruments are U.S. Treasury bills. These are issued in minimum denominations of $10,000 and auctioned every Monday. The large corporation's equivalent of the Treasury bill is high-grade commercial paper, which is usually issued in denominations of $25,000, and may be purchased through dealers or brokers. Negotiable certificates of deposit are the bank's Treasury bill equivalent. They carry a maturity of at least thirty days and the investor must make a minimum purchase of $100,000.

You may find it difficult to get your hands on these instruments. Obviously, you must have plenty of money to buy them. The organizations issuing them don't like to sell them to individual investors. And many brokers won't knock themselves out to get them for you because commissions are low and they can't make a living that way. Therefore the individual investor would do well to consider the excellent alternative presented by money market funds.

Money market funds are simply portfolios of money market instruments put together by an investment manager and made available to individual investors. When the individual investor buys one of these funds he enjoys almost all the

FIGURE 18

SELECTED MONEY MARKET FUNDS

Money market mutual funds	Assets (as of 9/19/74) millions of dollars	Minimum partici- pation	Load/ no-load
American General Reserve Fund (Houston)	$6.25	$5,000	load [1%]
Anchor Reserve Fund (Elizabeth, N.J.)	17.0	100	load [8¾%]
J. P. Cabot Short-term Fund (Valley Stream, N.Y.)	3.2	5,000	no-load
California Fund for Invest- ment in U.S. Government Securities (Fresno)	3.34	100	no-load
Capital Liquidity (L.A.)	0.65	3,000	no-load
Capital Preservation Fund (Palo Alto)	11.5	1,000	no-load
Current Interest Money Market Fund (Houston)	5.50	1,000	no-load
Daily Income Fund (N.Y.C.)	13.1	5,000	no-load
Dreyfus Liquid Assets (N.Y.C.)	372.0	5,000	no-load
Fidelity Daily Income Trust (Boston)	179.0	5,000	no-load
Holding Trust (Coral Gables, Fla.)	0.45	1,000	no-load
Kemper Income and Capital Preservation Fund (Chicago)	13.5	100	load [6%]
Money Market Management (Pittsburgh)	160.0	1,000	no-load
Oppenheimer Monetary Bridge (N.Y.C.)	20.0	1,000	load [4½%]
Reserve Fund (N.Y.C.)	365.0	5,000	no-load
STCM Corp. (N.Y.C.)	1.60	1,000	no-load
Scudder Managed Reserve (Boston)	29.19	1,000	no-load

benefits of owning the money market instruments himself. In addition, he avoids almost all their disadvantages.

Money market funds are highly liquid. They can be bought and sold daily. In general they can be bought in increments of as little as $1000. Interest accrues daily—seven days a week.

In some cases you can actually write checks on the money in your account. Fidelity Management & Research Company of Boston, Massachusetts, has set up such a fund. Your invested funds are easily accessible through a check-writing redemption system administered by National Shawmut Bank. Any time you like, you may write a check for $1000 or more on your funds, just as if they were in a regular checking account. And, on July 12, 1974, the fund was yielding 11.26 percent. Investors who put money into this fund seem to have found the best of all possible worlds: they are getting a high current interest rate on something that is very close to a checking account. At the same time they are participating in a diversified portfolio of money market instruments. And no matter how low the risks of default may be for any single issuer of certificates of deposit or commercial paper, the investor should always seek diversification if it comes at low or no cost. Figure 18 lists 17 relatively well-known money market funds in business at the end of 1974.

CASH MANAGEMENT RULE NO. 4

Avoid paying your bills for as long as possible. Don't be ashamed to flirt on the ragged edge of being a deadbeat. Corporate treasurers have learned that there can be big payoffs to the imaginative procrastinator. And if you can stall and do it with a lot of class, even your creditors will respect you, although they may not enjoy cooling their heels.

CASH MANAGEMENT RULE NO. 5

Become systematic as you receive your bills. There are some bills with no explicitly stated interest penalty. These go in the far-future payment file. Experience will tell you how far you can really push people. Push them as far as you can. Other bills will have an interest penalty, but if your check arrives only one month late, it is forgotten. Make sure your check arrives one month late. Finally, there are bills on which interest begins early, usually within twenty-five days, and is as much as 1½ percent a month. Pay these within the time period. Above all, use your credit card— never pay cash. The cost of credit is already figured in the price of the item. And almost nobody is giving discounts for cash these days.

You will never get rich by delaying bill payments. But do it anyway. It will give you the gall to ignore Poor Richard. It will put you in the same class as most millionaires, who are notorious procrastinators when it comes to paying bills. This is not the way they got rich but it is apparently part of their mentality.

Develop the same mental habits.

Ben Franklin once wrote: "Who goeth a-borrowing goeth a-sorrowing." But remember, like most public figures, he often wrote words meant for others—*not* for himself.

8

When Commodities Beat Inflation

The great inflation of 1973-74 brought on an age of commodities. People who didn't know soybeans from sorghum began to realize that there was a good chance to make money if the difference could be learned. And quick to jump at any opportunity, some investment advisers began to argue that just as the 1950s and 1960s were the golden age of stocks, the 1970s and the 1980s will be the age of commodities.

It is already history that commodities were a super investment play during 1973-74. Commodity price news moved from deep down in the financial pages to the front page. The reasons for the extraordinary performance of commodities are not so well known nor do they imply that a golden age of perpetually rising commodity prices is upon us. In fact, an analog of forces that pushed commodity prices up in 1973–74 could just as easily push them down. Most of the newspaper talk about rising commodity prices focused on limitations of supply—sometimes assumed to be perpetual—that would keep commodities permanently in the shortage category in the face of rising demand. Grains, it was argued, would continue scarce because of burgeoning demand in the so-called Third World, coupled with the impact of a twenty-year drought, on the capacity of temperate-zone agriculture to produce them. The outlook for high-protein animal feeds, soybeans for example, was assumed to be even more exciting because of the shift in world diet patterns toward meat as a result of prosperity. When it came to metals and oil, the problem was perceived to be monopoly power on the part of the less-developed countries. The Arab oil embargo was assumed to be followed by similar cartel actions on the part of bauxite producers, copper producers and other raw-material producers.

Supply constraints did play something of a role in 1973–74 commodity inflation. But more important, even though less publicized, was the ballooning of the world money supply in 1971 and 1972. Together with the several devaluations of the U.S. dollar, which made U.S. exports more attractive to foreigners, the surge in the world's money supply caused a surge in world output, which in turn led to an increase in the rate at which commodities were chewed up and to a surge in their prices.

Similarly, the decline in commodity prices which occurred in the first half of 1975 was the result of the drop in the world money growth rate that occurred in 1973 and 1974. As with every other investment, the *Beat Inflation* investor will time his commodity purchases to swings in the money supply.

The time to buy commodities is in the accelerating phase of the inflation cycle; it is the only time to buy commodities. And even if you expect inflation to accelerate, you still have to be very careful. This is so even though the accelerating inflation of 1973–74 gave commodities a bright new look— and as a consequence made many brokerage houses which normally push their stock business attempt to get investors to consider commodities as an alternative. Like other companies, brokerage houses try to push business in one line when they are losing it in other lines. And now that these brokerage houses have built up their commodities departments they are going to continue to push commodities.

The kinds of stories that salesmen tell are going to be breathtaking. The price of soybeans rose from $4.21 per bushel to $8.30 between January 4, 1973, and August 23, 1973. The price of wheat from $2.71 per bushel to $4.99 per bushel. Cotton from 34.18 cents per pound to 76.35 cents per pound.

Commodity contracts, moreover, are almost always bought on margin. Thin margin. With a 10 percent margin requirement, the right timing on investment decisions would have turned $10,000 into $197,150 in soybeans, $184,133 in wheat, and $223,376 in cotton.* These heady examples could be duplicated in almost every commodity.

What happened over the next seven months is also worth knowing. Soybeans skidded by 27.1 percent between August 23, 1973, and March 28, 1974; wheat by 12.3 percent; cotton by 15.7 percent. Investors who put in their $10,000 around the time the peaks were reached would have been wiped out quickly.

Low margin requirements and wide price swings make commodity investment the next thing to shooting craps in Las Vegas. Those who want to beat the commodities game must be supersensitive to the very first indication of a change in the inflation rate. The general rules for spotting a change in the inflation rate are outlined in Chapter 2. To capitalize on commodity price changes, the *Beat Inflation* investor must be certain that he understands the inflation early-warning system completely. He must receive a clear and certain signal that the inflation rate is about to change. If he has any doubts, the best advice we can give is to stay away. There is no trick at all to getting bagged in commodities.

The reason is that the man on the other side of the commodities transaction is likely to be a real pro. The commodity market in which the ordinary investor trades is a futures

---

* This is somewhat of an oversimplification. Every futures contract is for a specific quantity determined by the Commodity Exchange.

market; it exists primarily because the real pros, the baking companies that need wheat, the feedlot operators who need soybeans, do not want to take the risk that wide fluctuations in price will drive them out of business. So when you buy or sell commodities futures you tread where the pros themselves fear to tread; the commodity futures markets exist because the companies that use commodities do not wish to take the risk of price fluctuations. So it should not be surprising that the average investor loses on commodity futures far more often than he gains according to authoritative studies.

To avoid sharing the fate of the multitude, investors must proceed warily. But there may nevertheless be times when those who like to gamble will have the odds stacked in their favor. Those investors guided by the following six rules will have a fighting chance of making a triple play: finding the right commodity, finding the right period, and finding the right transaction—a buy or a sell.

COMMODITY RULE NO. 1

Buy commodities only in the accelerating phase of the inflation cycle. The purchase should be timed so that it occurs early in this phase. Commodity prices are the first place that accelerating inflation shows itself, well before the newspapers tell you that a rise in the cost of living is making housewives unhappy or unions restless. It is just as easy to sell commodities for future delivery as it is to buy them. Those investors who can spot an early deceleration in the inflation rate have a chance to sell commodities and make big profits. For example, on August 7, 1974, you could have sold soybeans for future delivery on January 9, 1975, at $8.47 per bushel. When January 9 rolled around, you could have honored your contract by buying soybeans in the spot market for $6.70 and pocketed the difference. This kind of play should only be made early in the decelerating phase of the inflation cycle, the earlier in the phase the better.

COMMODITY RULE NO. 2

Only make a commitment to commodities when the change in the inflation rate that you expect will be major and is largely unanticipated by the general public.

When the commodities future salesman starts to call you, the first thing he will do is to ask you if you would like to receive a bunch of booklets detailing all the factors that influence the price of each commodity. These booklets will also tell you what clues to watch for as to future price movements.

For example, a sample of the literature distributed by the Chicago Mercantile Exchange, one of the more aggressive and better commodities exchanges in the world, illustrates the kinds of factors you, the commodity investor, would have to be on top of.

> As an example of the factors to consider, the cattle speculator should check cattle-on-feed reports, cattle slaughter and beef production, beef consumption, the calf crop, feed prices, weather conditions in livestock states, and shipments of feeder cattle, among other livestock figures.
>
> Pork belly and live hog facts of interest would include cold storage stocks, hog slaughter, sliced bacon production, and pig crop reports which include breeding intentions and inventory of hogs on farms.
>
> Copper supply is determined by a number of factors, among them reserves of copper stocks, amount of and potential for increasing production capacity, technological innovations, and temporary blockages of supply flows. The alert analyst should consider all of these factors, some of which are more important in the short-run, others being more significant in the long-term considerations.
>
> Demand for copper is determined by a number of factors, some of the most important of which are desirability of holding valuable metals, industrial demand for copper, and the substitutability of other materials.

According to the booklets there are 24 factors to consider for cattle, 24 for pork bellies, and 28 for copper. Following any one of these commodities would obviously be a full-time job. It would take a lifetime, probably starting with some technical education, to really get good at it. And remember that, as a commodity speculator, you are betting against the pros, who are hedging. You can also be sure that those with specialized knowledge have exploited every obvious profit opportunity.

The only thing that the *Beat Inflation* investor has going for him is his ability to forecast the inflation rate. And to beat the pros he must expect a major swing in the inflation rate. If the swing isn't big, the price of any commodity is likely to be more influenced by special factors—weather conditions in the Midwest, rainfall in Nigeria, hoof-and-mouth disease in Argentina, and the like—than by moderate changes in the general inflation rate.

In the case of pork bellies, Swift and Company and the other meat packers have large staffs and specialized information systems to find out what will happen to prices. It is therefore highly unlikely that you will be the first to know when the fundamental conditions change. *The point of all this for the* Beat Inflation *investor is that the only chance of beating the pros is when the swing in the inflation rate is major and largely unanticipated.*

COMMODITY RULE NO. 3

Diversification applies to commodities just as it applies to everything else. Even with a big and largely unanticipated swing in the inflation rate, specialized factors could still make your commodity investment look very bad.

There is a futures market for shell eggs. A single contract calls for 750 cases of 30 dozen each, which translates into 22,500 dozens or 270,000 fresh, large white eggs. When you buy those eggs you had better make sure you can sell them.

If you eat one egg per day it would take you almost 740 years to consume them.

Suppose the Surgeon General of the United States releases a report that clearly demonstrates a positive and direct link between heart disease and egg consumption. Or that the link between cholesterol in eggs and heart disease is even closer than was indicated by previous research. If your monetary indicators had told you that inflation was about to accelerate and you put all your commodity money in the egg basket, you would get wiped out even though you were 100 percent right about the commodity inflation. The moral of the story is not to put all your eggs in one basket. Going back to the principles of investment outlined in Chapter 4, remember it always pays to diversify. Buy several commodities or a mutual fund that holds a diversified portfolio of contracts.

COMMODITY RULE NO. 4

Always bear in mind that gold is just another commodity. Contrary to what the Johnny One-Notes may say, gold is not a surefire hedge against inflation. As a matter of fact, now that governments no longer seriously peg the price of gold, and U.S. citizens can buy it, its price has become supersensitive to changes in the inflation rate. So be supercareful, because there is a huge gold inventory out there. Virtually all the gold ever produced is still in existence. Central bankers alone hold 1.2 billion ounces.

Moreover, gold is useless—it heats no homes, feeds nobody, and earns no income. Central bankers will be highly tempted to sell it in a world faced with big oil-related balance-of-payments deficits. In fact, in late 1974 the U.S. Government decided to auction some of its gold hoard. At some point, other governments will also dump gold. Then look out, because the effect on gold prices could be even greater than the impact of the discovery of a stronger linkage between egg consumption and heart disease on the price of shell eggs.

COMMODITY RULE No. 5

Stay away from exotic commodities like wine and art. Specialized knowledge is even more important here than in such prosaic things as cocoa and soybeans. If you are selling a painting, you may not be able to find a buyer without incurring a catastrophic sacrifice in price. Artists move in and out of fashion much more rapidly than do lead and zinc. The art market, moreover, depends very much on the financial conditions of museums, which in turn depend on gift tax laws in a few countries. These can and do change.

Wine is for drinking, not for speculation. While it might be nice to time the wine purchases for your cellar so as to take advantage of lower prices, don't plan on selling out when prices go up. You are likely to miss the peak and incur high middleman charges.

Prices of exotic investments move up as well as down, but there are far better ways to play the inflation cycle.

COMMODITY RULE No. 6

Stay away from high-priced coins produced by the Franklin Mint and other private "mints." The Franklin Mints of the world came into being because U.S. citizens have not up to now been allowed to hold gold in its pure form. They have flourished by mixing gold with other metals and engraving pictures on the resulting alloy. There has to be a big mark-up over the price of gold. Someone is paying Franklin Mint's promotion-campaign bills, among other things. Unless the price of gold really soars, the game that the Franklin Mints of the world are asking you to play can only be won by their stockholders. Their baubles can't be sold by you except at a loss. And you can use only so many as paperweights.

Stamps and old coins should be collected only by those who actually enjoy this kind of thing—not as an inflation hedge. They may rise in price during the accelerating phase of the inflation but, as in the case of wine, there is a big spread between the buying and the selling price. Just for fun, go in and see what a dealer will offer you for your stamp collection. Don't just ask him to appraise it; ask him how much cash he will give you for it.

These rules indicate that commodity plays are a much tougher row to hoe than the more traditional kinds of investment vehicles. Unless you get your kicks directly from them, you are better off to stay away under most circumstances. To make money in the commodities market you need a big, unanticipated swing in the inflation rate and you have to get in there early. The year 1973 did present such an opportunity to buy commodity contracts, and 1974 was a good time to sell commodity contracts—but opportunities such as these rarely occur.

9

What Currencies
Should You Hold?

Currencies float these days, and this opens up a whole new world for the investor. Prior to the summer of 1971 governments kept the price of their currencies fixed in terms of the dollar, and therefore in terms of all other currencies. Sometimes governments were forced to change the price of their currency but the timing of these changes was spasmodic and highly unpredictable. Furthermore, when the changes finally came they were mammoth. The value of a currency could change by as much as 10 to 20 percent in one day.

But now that currencies are floating, they change in price relative to each other by fairly small amounts every day, much as common stocks and bonds do. There are still extra political risks in investing in currencies but they have become a much more reasonable investment play.

In fact, you don't have to deal with the gnomes of Zurich to play them. In recent years currencies have become as easy to play as commodities. The International Monetary Market of the Chicago Mercantile Exchange is a place where you can buy a standardized contract for the pound sterling, Canadian dollar, German mark, Dutch guilder, Japanese yen, Mexican peso and Swiss franc as easily as you can buy 100 shares of General Motors. In fact, your friendly local broker is likely to be dealing in currency futures. Just like stocks, currencies have their own ticker symbols. For example, the British pound has the symbol BP, the Canadian dollar CD, and so on. A standard contract for, say, the British pound is for 25,000 pounds or approximately $60,000 U.S. dollars. The minimum fluctuation on a sterling contract is approximately .0005, or $30.00.

Like the commodities market, the currencies market is a dangerous play. In 1974 the newspapers were full of stories about banks that got into trouble because a foreign-exchange trader stepped out of line. This was one of the primary reasons the Franklin National Bank had severe problems in the United States, why the Bankhaus Herstatt went bust in Germany, and why the Swiss branch of the prestigious Lloyds Bank of London got into deep trouble.

One of the few sayings for which the nineteenth-century financier J. P. Morgan was famous is applicable here. When a young man asked him what would happen to stocks, he replied, "Son, they will fluctuate." It is easy to see why Morgan became a tycoon. And anybody who wants to invest for profit must also remember that gold, bonds, short-term money instruments, commodities and currencies all have their downs as well as their ups.

The Japanese yen provides a graphic example. Thought to be indestructible in 1972, the yen began to tumble in 1973 and fell on its rear end in 1974. On the average, you would have gotten 265 yen to the dollar in September of 1973, but one year later you would have gotten 300 yen to the dollar. This means that the man who bought 265,000 yen at the average price of the first quarter of 1973 for $1000, would have gotten $883 for his 265,000 yen and his trouble at the average price that prevailed during September of 1974. And if, as is more likely, our currency speculator had used his money to buy a forward contract for yen on the Chicago International Monetary Market and had used margin, he probably would have been sold out of his position and have a lot less than $883 per $1000 to show for it.

What happened to the yen? The oil embargo and the subsequent quadrupling of the oil price did cause special problems for the Japanese. A huge percentage of their oil needs are satisfied by Middle East sources. But the oil price was quadrupled for everybody. And the most general explanation of the sinking yen was a Japanese inflation rate that made United States double-digit inflation look like price stability. At the beginning of 1973 Japanese wholesale price inflation was running at a 9.3 percent annual rate, U.S. wholesale price inflation at an 8.6 percent annual rate. By the first quarter of 1974, Japanese wholesale price inflation was at a 35.5 percent annual rate, that of the U.S. at a 17.4 percent annual rate. A similar comparison made for consumer prices shows that the Japanese inflation rate went from 7.2 percent to 24.2 percent, while the U.S. consumer price inflation went from 4.1 percent to 9.9 percent. The yen sank relative to the dollar mainly because the Japanese inflation rate soared above the U.S. inflation rate. We could endlessly repeat stories of changing currency values from every epoch in history. However, the conclusion is always the same: The countries that have the fastest inflation always see the price of their currency sink compared to the currencies of countries that have relatively little inflation. Opportunities to make money in currencies will therefore occur when anticipated inflation rates, as incorporated in the price of foreign exchange, get way out of line with what the *Beat Inflation* investor himself expects. The difficulty is in spotting these situations. To help you develop a strategy for uncovering currencies whose prices are out of whack with probable future inflation rates there are six *Beat Inflation* rules.

CURRENCY RULE NO. 1

Buy a country's currency in the wake of a sharp deceleration of the country's monetary growth rate; sell a currency
in the wake of a sharp acceleration in a country's monetary
growth rate.

When a country's monetary growth rate accelerates sharply
it is a signal that higher inflation rates are down the road.
Faster monetary growth will translate itself into an intensi-
fied decline in the purchasing power of that currency, not
only with respect to domestic goods, but also with respect
to the amount of foreign goods it can command. When
money accelerates, prices go up, not only at home but also
for goods produced for sale in the world market. Moreover,
imports from countries not experiencing so rapid an inflation begin to look cheap. Thus, when money growth moves
up, exports are hit on the head and imports soar. In the
world money markets, rising inflation for a country dooms
its currency to fall. Falling exports reduce the demand for
that currency, and rising imports increase the supply.

CURRENCY RULE NO. 2

In world currency markets it is the relative inflation rate
that really counts. A country's currency should be bought if
you expect that country to experience a lower inflation rate
than other countries. It should be sold if you expect it to
experience a higher inflation rate than other countries. Remember, if you are to make any money, your expectations
have to differ markedly from those of average opinion in the
marketplace.

The behavior of the Japanese yen during 1973 and 1974
represented a classic instance where Rules One and Two
could have been put into action to outwit average opinion
in the currency market. Early in 1973 opinion that the Japanese yen would rise sharply was widespread. But, the *Beat*

Inflation investor would have foreseen a sharp relative acceleration in the Japanese price level because he would have noticed a sharp acceleration of Japanese monetary growth in 1972. He would then have been led to expect a fall in the yen relative to the currencies of those countries where monetary growth was not accelerating. And fall the yen did. The comparison to the dollar is instructive. The Federal Reserve put on a good show of monetary restraint as compared to the Bank of Japan, the Japanese Central Bank. It happened in fits and starts. But the differences in the monetary growth rates did lead to a fall in the yen relative to the dollar. All the classic elements of a profitable currency play were there for the yen versus the dollar. In early 1973 the market expected the yen to stay strong. But the *Beat Inflation* investor knew it was fated to weaken.

When this kind of divergence between the opinion of the *Beat Inflation* investor and average opinion occurs, it's cornucopia time. One word of warning: Because of institutional differences in the rate at which money turns over, there will always be differences in the size of the monetary growth rates between countries. What really matters in making money in the currency market is the acceleration and deceleration in the country's own monetary growth rate. What was important for the yen versus the dollar was that the Japanese monetary growth rate jumped while the U.S. monetary growth rate declined.

The 1973 Nobel Prize for monetary restraint went to Germany and Switzerland, and their inflation rates fared the best in 1974. To be certain, the currency markets already had great respect for the German mark and Swiss franc. Both countries had a good record in combating inflation. To preserve this good record in the face of world-wide commodity price pressures, these countries really slammed on the monetary brakes. Observing this, the *Beat Inflation* investor would have expected Swiss and German inflation rates to come down faster than in other countries. He would, therefore, have been able to see before everybody else the rise in the Swiss franc and German mark that took place.

Given the monetary growth rates of Germany, Switzerland and Japan, the best currency play was to borrow yen and buy Swiss francs and German marks. The safest thing to do is always bet against the currency with biggest acceleration in its monetary growth rate and in favor of the currency with the smallest acceleration or, even better, biggest deceleration. But beware. If some investors jump on a currency that the *Beat Inflation* investor also believes is fundamentally sound because the country has a "good" monetary growth rate and thus a low future inflation rate, its price can be driven out of sight. Before going whole hog for the German mark, Dutch guilder or the Swiss franc remember that even a sound currency can become overpriced if average opinion is reflecting too sanguine a view of the country's inflation rate as compared to inflation rates in other countries.

CURRENCY RULE NO. 3

Currency plays as outlined above should only be made when there is a major shift in the monetary growth rate. Smaller movements can easily be swamped by other unpredictable factors.

Under the discussion of Commodity Rule No. 1, the *Beat Inflation* investor was warned to stay away from commodity plays unless he foresaw a major change in the monetary growth rate that would be strong enough to push all prices upward. The reason was that each commodity's price depended not only on the general rate of inflation but also on some very special demand and supply factors. It was also pointed out that when you invest in commodities you are going into a market where the professionals themselves fear to tread.

What is true of commodities is also true of currencies. Currency values will depend not only on the inflation rate in a particular country compared to the inflation in other countries but also on special factors. The world of international trade and finance, moreover, is horrendously complex. People who spend their lifetime studying it get themselves excited about such concepts as the liquidity balance of payments, the balance of trade, and the official settlements balance of payments. But, most important, unlike the commodities market, Central Banks fiddle in the currency markets and can upset or delay the workings of the fundamentals. In fact, they can really blow your investment strategy to smithereens. Thus, if a knowledge of the *Beat Inflation* strategy is to prove helpful in currency trading, the swing in the monetary growth rate must be big enough so that it provides strong odds that other factors will be swamped.

CURRENCY RULE NO. 4

Don't ignore weak currencies; they may offer excellent opportunities to make money.

When a currency falls into disfavor the market tends to be too pessimistic about its outlook. Moreover, economic difficulties push even the most recalcitrant governments into some action to bring their inflation rate under control.

Given the influence of the Johnny One-Notes who tend to talk up the hard currencies, and therefore bid up their price, the *Beat Inflation* investor may easily find the best currency plays among countries that are generally considered to be weak sisters. So the *Beat Inflation* investor should keep his eye riveted on such historically weak currencies as Italy and Britain for the signs of a switch toward restraint in monetary policy.

CURRENCY RULE NO. 5

When you buy the stocks of multinational companies it is desirable to buy companies that have good sales penetration in those countries whose currencies you expect to be strong. This rule could have been stated as a stock rule but it is much more practical here, now that you understand why currencies fluctuate.

Following this rule will not make you rich but it could give you an extra edge under certain circumstances. When you consider the stock of a multinational company in a certain industry, it is worth observing where its sales are concentrated. Then look to see what the exchange market is saying about the prospects for that country's currency. Whatever the exchange market is saying will be reflected in the price of the stock. So that, if you expect the currency of the country where sales are concentrated to do better than what average opinion believes, the stock will have an element of undervaluation from the *Beat Inflation* point of view. Currency expectations are not of themselves important reasons to pick a stock. But if you do make investments in multinational companies, keep them in mind.

CURRENCY RULE NO. 6

You can use the currency plays rules to increase your return from holding short-term money market instruments in other countries. The other side of this rule is to use currency plays to reduce your net interest costs when you are borrowing money abroad. Right now Currency Rule No. 6 is only for the corporate treasurer since the individual will have a tough time borrowing from foreign financial institutions. But this may change.

When you buy money market instruments abroad, the return you get will depend on the relationship between the price of foreign currency when you buy the instrument and the price of the currency when you sell it. Well-informed investors will be aware of the differences in interest rates between countries, and that these differences will reflect the market's view of how exchange rates will change. For example, Swiss interest rates will be low compared to those in other countries if the market expects the Swiss franc to go up. This is because the total return to the holder of a Swiss money market instrument will include not only the interest yield but also some foreign exchange profit. To a foreign investor this means that he can expect a relatively low interest rate if he can be reasonably sure that the Swiss francs he gets when the instrument matures will be worth more than when he made his original purchase.

When world money markets are relatively free, the total return to investing in money market instruments tends toward equality. Those countries with relatively high monetary growth rates will have high interest rates and there will be a general expectation that their currencies will be weak. The countries with relatively low monetary growth rates will have low interest rates, and there will be a general expectation that their currencies will strengthen. To put Currency Rule No. 6 into practice, you must have markedly different expectations than generally prevail in the exchange markets. If you notice, for example, a sharp deceleration in some country's monetary growth and the exchange market does not reflect it adequately, the time may be at hand.

Currency Rule No. 6, for example, would have suggested that British Treasury bills were a good investment in the third quarter of 1973. At that time their average yield was 11 percent as against 8.3 percent for U.S. Treasury bills of equivalent maturity. By the third quarter of 1973 it was apparent that Britain had already applied the monetary brakes, and this made it apparent to the *Beat Inflation* investor that the pound would improve. At that time this would have been a contrary opinion, since the average expectation was that Britain would sink slowly into the sea, dragging the pound down with it. As it turned out, the pound did improve in 1974, so the *Beat Inflation* investor would have been able to obtain a juicy current yield plus a neat foreign exchange gain.

In the above transaction, the *Beat Inflation* investor was a lender. It also is possible to increase your total return by borrowing in those countries where you expect the currency to weaken substantially. The *Beat Inflation* borrowing game requires that you do just the opposite of what you did when you were playing *Beat Inflation* by buying money market instruments. If you see a country's monetary growth rate accelerating sharply, its banks and capital markets are a good place to borrow money. If the market does not reflect the full impact of the monetary spurt going on in a country, its currency will probably be overvalued and its interest rates too low. This will give you an opportunity to keep the total cost of borrowing very low.

The situation in Japan in the first half of 1973 presents a classic example. Borrowers lucky enough to have access to the Japanese market were able to get credit at a little over 6 percent; at the same time the Bank of Japan, the Japanese Central Bank, was running wild, pushing the monetary growth rate up at an annual rate of more than 25 percent. Using our currency rules, the *Beat Inflation* investor should have expected a decline in the yen. This did occur. In September of 1973 a dollar bought 265 yen. By September of 1974 it bought about 300 yen. Vis-à-vis the dollar, the yen declined by almost 12 percent on a quarterly average basis. Thus, the American who was lucky enough to have borrowed yen would have actually paid no interest. A 6 percent one-year loan means that the man who had borrowed 265 yen would have to pay 281 yen back at the end of one year. Since you could buy 300 yen for a dollar, the borrower would have benefited enough from changes in the exchange rate to more than offset his interest costs. The *Beat Inflation* investor who can spot this kind of situation should not heed Beneficial Finance's advice; when a country's monetary growth rate accelerates very sharply he both can and should "borrow money needlessly" there.

Over the years, the ability of the ordinary investor to make currency plays has been limited by exchange and capital controls and a predisposition on the part of central banks to fix their exchange rates. But the change to a floating rate system has clearly widened opportunities to benefit from exchange rate differences between countries. But beware. Central bankers are creatures of habit. They like to meddle and this will lead to periods when the floating rate system gets dirty. That is to say, central bankers will attempt to prevent the fundamental forces that we have been describing from operating, at least temporarily. This increases the risk in using the foreign exchange markets as a *Beat Inflation* vehicle.

It is therefore prudent to play the foreign exchange markets only when there is a very wide divergence from what market participants generally expect and what the *Beat Inflation* rules say will happen.

Exchange controls still exist around the world, and this limits the extent to which individual investors can use the currency rules. However, controls are not as tough as they used to be, and more important for the individual investor is the development of a good futures market in currencies on the Chicago Mercantile Exchange.

10

Indexing: Your Job, Pension, and Social Security

High, volatile and permanent inflation isn't only changing the investment environment; it is also changing every aspect of your economic life: the way you get paid, the way you accrue pension rights and even the way in which the Social Security Administration figures how big a check it is going to send you when you are over sixty-five.

The omnibus name for the kinds of change that permanent inflation is bringing to daily economic life is "indexing." The name is new in the United States but the underlying idea is broadly familiar. Any time an agreement or contract is concluded and contains provisions tying the size of payments to some measure of the inflation rate, indexing is present. Cost-of-living clauses have been around for a long time in union contracts. Workers demanded and received them during earlier bouts of inflation but they tended to fall into disuse when prices again became stable. But now that inflation is permanent, indexing will become a permanent part of your economic life and a household word.

You should think about when and when not to enter into indexed contracts, what kinds of agreements to index and what kinds of agreements not to index, what kinds of price indexes to use for escalator clauses and when in the inflation cycle indexing best serves to *Beat Inflation*.

Indexing is one of those things that is most easily grasped by taking a look at some escalator contracts in action. For example, the 1973–76 wage agreement between the General Electric Company and the International Union of Electrical, Radio and Machine Workers includes a cost-of-living adjustment tied to price changes. The formula used to calculate the size of the cost-of-living adjustment is as follows: "one cent (1¢) per hour for hourly employees, forty cents (40¢) per week for salaried employees for each full three tenths of one percent (0.3%) by which the National Consumer Price Index (1967=100), as published by the United States Bureau of Labor Statistics, increases in the applicable measurement period."

The authors laid their hands on this example by asking Nat Goldfinger, Director of Research for the AFL-CIO, for an example of a cost-of-living escalator that is good from labor's point of view. Even so, the formula allows the worker to capture only 80 percent of the rise in the consumer price index.

This is an extremely generous contract—well above average as a study in the July, 1974, Federal Reserve Bank of New York *Monthly Review* shows. The study points out that the consumer price index rose at a 5.3 annual rate between 1968 and 1973. Over the same period the average cost-of-living wage increase came to just 2.7 percent per year; so that even those workers covered by cost-of-living escalator clauses managed only about a 50 percent protection against inflation.

Cost-of-living contracts are still far from universal, even in the labor movement. By the end of 1973, approximately 4 million workers, only about 40 percent of the workers under contract, were covered by escalator clauses, so that the unions which have gone the farthest in getting cost-of-living clauses still have a long way to go in obtaining full inflation protection for their members—at least through cost-of-living clauses.

There is no data on what percentage of the total work force has some sort of a cost-of-living protection built into their salaries. But it is small, too small, for a world of high and volatile inflation. If you don't have a cost-of-living escalator, get one whenever you can.

Actually, high and volatile inflation makes it necessary to change the way in which you think about your job. No one enjoys a job in which the only reward is the size of the paycheck. And inflation should not change your desire for work that is meaningful and brings nonfinancial rewards. But be this as it may, it is worth getting every cent you can out of your boss. And here are four rules that can help you get the best cost-of-living protection that you can. Everybody recognizes that there is less individual freedom in striking job bargains than in investing. But with imagination and guts you may find that you can make these rules work for you.

JOB RULE NO. 1

Get your wage expressed in terms of its purchasing power. Make sure that you don't suffer inflation shock. Keep in mind at all times how fast prices are rising so you know exactly how well you are doing on the wage and salary front. You may like your boss, but remember the old trade union saying that "all bosses is bastards"; it is in the nature of being a boss. So it is a fair game to use your *Beat Inflation* knowledge to strike a deal that is advantageous to you. Remember the farmers and their famous parity index. You want parity too. There are local consumer price indexes as well as one for the whole nation. A call to your local office of the Bureau of Labor Statistics will get you on the mailing list for the monthly press release that tells you about changes in the local consumer price index. This index, with all its faults, is still the best instrument around for measuring the way your cost of living is changing. A deal with your boss that gives you good cost-of-living protection will guarantee that your salary will rise by the same percentage as the change in local cost of living—so that if you succeed in getting it tied to changes in the local cost of living you will have succeeded in expressing your wage in terms of its purchasing power. This is full indexing and is better than the best union contract. Try to get it.

JOB RULE NO. 2

Make sure that the cost-of-living adjustments come frequently. The faster the inflation rate, the more frequent the adjustments should be. Time is money. The more frequently you get your cost-of-living adjustment, the better off you are. During the great German inflation of the 1920s, workers were paid twice a day because prices were much higher in the afternoon than in the morning. Things are not that bad here, nor are they likely to be. But price changes are big enough so that those who can get monthly or even quarterly cost-of-living adjustments are materially better off than those who have to wait till the end of the year.

Don't let your wages trail; minimize the wage lag. Consumer prices rose by about 12 percent in 1974. Had your agreement with your boss called for a full cost-of-living adjustment at the end of the year, it would not have done you a bit of good during 1974. Maintaining your car, paying your utility bills and setting food on the family table would have left you strapped. You would have been much better able to cope had your wage escalation showed up in your pay check quickly. Suppose, for example, that your initial salary was $20,000 per year or $5,000 per quarter. A 12 percent rate of price increase means 3 percent per quarter, so that if you had a quarterly escalation you would have gotten paid $21,545.68 during the year. That extra $1545.68 that you would have received during the year would have bought meat and potatoes that you would not otherwise have had.

JOB RULE NO. 3

To jack up the amount you earn over the course of your working life, make your job changes during the accelerating phase of the inflation cycle. Unless you have really been able to put Job Rule No. 2 to your boss, the odds are that your wage will stand still and your purchasing power decline when prices shoot up in the accelerating phase of the inflation cycle. This is not the only reason why the accelerating phase of the inflation cycle is the right time to change jobs. Usually the early upswing in the inflation cycle will be accompanied by booming business, so that companies will be willing to pay more to get new workers on board. Employees already on the staff may someday catch up but ordinarily it will take them some time to do so.

JOB RULE NO. 4

The decelerating phase of the inflation cycle may be a good time to stay where you are. When price increases start to slow, business conditions are generally soft and unemployment is rising. Sending around résumés is apt to be pointless. A sick job market is no place to generate much in the way of salary increases. At the same time, it is quite possible that things will be changing at the place you are already working in a way that is quite favorable to those able to hang onto their jobs. If there is any wage lag at all in your company it is quite likely that the employees will be catching up with past inflation rates during the decelerating phase of the inflation cycle. When inflation is decelerating your present job may be the best plan to maximize your income.

The rules that will maximize your job income will also tend to maximize your pension benefits. In American industry, pension payments are ordinarily based on some formula that ties them to your average salary in your last five years of employment—so that if you have done the right thing to get your salary up, your pension will follow it up.

But beware. No matter how good a job you do in negotiating for your pension, the chances are that it will provide inadequate benefits in a world of high and volatile inflation. To make things worse, Social Security may not turn out to be the cornucopia it is touted to be, particularly if you are young right now. With benefit increases that have occurred over the past three years, and with the indexing of future payments to changes in the cost of living, Social Security is delivering a lot to those currently in retirement and is likely to continue delivering a lot to those who will enter retirement in the next few years. But problems will start to show in the mid-1980s. And that is not too far away when you are thinking about investing for the future. Remember, the Social Security system is not funded. Whatever the defects of your company's pension plan may be, the new 1974 pension law requires that your pension benefits be fully funded at all times. This means that the money that you put in and the money that the boss puts in on your behalf is sequestered in a trust fund, so that if the firm goes bankrupt, your benefits will receive a measure of protection. The law also requires that the trust fund be big enough at all times to pay all the benefits that you have accumulated. So when you get your quarterly statement of the benefits you have accumulated you can have a fair degree of faith that they will actually be paid. In fact, the government has set up an insurance plan that means Uncle Sam will pay any benefits due you that the company can't pay.

Polls show that Americans have enormous faith in the Social Security system. But unlike your funded pension benefits, the Social Security system is what economists call a tax transfer system. In any given year the benefits paid to retirees are derived from taxes on those who are working.

Benefits have shot up over the past few years since the number of people employed has been going up more rapidly than the number of people retiring.

So it has been easy for the government to raise benefits. But the birth rate has now slumped and is likely to continue to be depressed. This means that there will be a continuous deterioration in the ability of the people who are working to support either their parents or somebody else's parents via Social Security. To many experts, this makes the promises of high future Social Security benefits suspect. This is just another reason why the *Beat Inflation* investor does not put all his eggs in one basket, even if that basket is the hallowed Social Security system. To insure a comfortable retirement, everybody must have his own investment program. And in a world of high and volatile inflation that program must be based on the *Beat Inflation* rules.

11

Choosing a Money Manager

If you decide you don't have the time to manage money yourself, you can use *Beat Inflation* to help you pick the right people to manage your money for you.

A world of high and volatile inflation obviously changes the ground rules by which money is to be managed. In this book we have spelled out a set of rules through which investment decisions can be geared to a world of permanent inflation. Other investment pros may come up with other approaches, and these may work as well as or even better than ours will. But for any money manager to succeed in beating inflation, he must clearly adapt his investment strategy to taking advantage of the ways in which inflation transfers income and wealth. All money managers will say that they have come to grips with inflation. Before you entrust your life savings to them, make sure they can prove it.

Getting a money manager who understands how inflation changes the investment environment is not going to be easy. Everybody knows it is hard to find a good doctor or dentist. The ethics of these professions make it hard to come by relevant information. Investment managers can't bury their mistakes—but they will do everything they possibly can to avoid paying for their mistakes. And the most obvious thing they do to accomplish this is to make their portfolios look as much like everybody else's portfolio as possible. By definition, this leads to almost everybody's showing the same mistakes as well as the same successes. As a consequence the standard money-management brochures, as well as other standard information sources, will not be of much help in finding the right person to manage your money in a world of high and variable inflation. Therefore, if you need professional money-management advice, you are going to have to do some real digging to find the right person or organization.

We have written this book so that you should be able to manage your own money. But even if you don't have the time or the temperament, you can nevertheless use your understanding of the inflation process to get better investment results. Just as the book can be used to manage your own money, it can also be used to help you pick the right money manager. Consequently, we have developed five questions that will allow you to separate those investment managers who have a good chance of beating inflation from those who don't.

MONEY MANAGEMENT QUESTION NO. 1

Is your money-management organization willing to invest in all assets? Money-management brochures, including those put out by mutual funds, more often than not will say that the organization leaves open the option to invest in any kind of asset deemed suitable for making the investor's capital grow. If you examine what these organizations do, however, the record will show that they stick to one or two investment vehicles. And if respectability is part of the image they seek to project, those vehicles are ordinarily stocks, bonds, and short-term money market instruments. And even this restricted list of potential investment vehicles projects an image of flexibility that doesn't really exist. The reason is that shifts between, say, cash and stocks tend to be small and occur for the wrong reason. For example, anyone who visited a respectable money manager during the 1973–74 stock market debacle would have been told that the organization had made a big move into cash. Chances are that this was true for bad reasons rather than good reasons. Suppose the organization had come into 1973 with 10 percent of its funds in short-term money market instruments and 90 percent in common stocks. Further, suppose that all the organization did was roll over its short-term money market instruments and watch the value of the common stocks go down. By fall of 1974 the value of its common stocks would have been down some 42½ percent and the value of its cash equivalents would have been unchanged. Therefore, by the fall of 1974, cash would have been 16.2 percent of the assets, and common stocks would have been 83.8 percent. This is one heck of a way to go into cash.

This kind of nonflexibility flexibility is going to be the fate of any investment manager who loves the same asset at all times over the entire inflation cycle. The period during which any vehicle will be a shining star will be brief. Accordingly your investment manager must do more than say he considers all assets. He must acutally invest in them at the right time.

Finding a money manager who treats all assets with equal justice and "fine impartiality" will be extremely difficult, and not only because of a commission structure that is still torqued in favor of common stocks. Cultural lag and the pressure of conventional wisdom continue to make investment managers, the press and even Congress think of some assets as respectable and some as odious and sinister. During 1973–74, many big bank trust departments sat around and watched the value of their common stock pension funds fall by 30 to 40 percent. People were upset with this performance but there were few lawsuits against the banks, no Congressional investigations of what happened, and no serious legislative remedy attempted. The reason seems to be that bonds and stocks, even though they got creamed, had more appeal to Poor Richard's ghost than other assets did.

Had the major institutions turned in the same investment performance with a portfolio of gold, Japanese yen and shell egg futures, heads would have rolled.

An asset is an asset is an asset. It will be hard for the *Beat Inflation* investor to do, but he must find a money manager whose attitude toward assets is determined solely by their appropriateness to the specific stage of the inflation cycle in which the economy finds itself.

MONEY MANAGEMENT QUESTION No. 2

Does your money-management organization structure its portfolios to reflect its knowledge of the future inflation rate and its impact on asset prices? It is not enough to be willing to invest in all assets. The money manager must have a framework for picking the appropriate vehicle for each stage of the inflation cycle. This book has described one method; other methods may be available. Make sure your money manager has a method and that the method makes sense to you. Portfolios that do not consider the income and wealth transfers that inflation brings are doomed to perform poorly.

MONEY MANAGEMENT QUESTION No. 3

How does your organization make its projections of the future inflation rate? The success of any *Beat Inflation* program is importantly dependent on the investor's or the investment manager's success in forecasting changes in the rate of inflation. Disastrous investment performance comes about from having the wrong assets for the particular phase of the inflation cycle. Nothing could be worse than a portfolio optimally designed to take advantage of decelerating inflation in a period when the inflation rate starts accelerating.

Beware the money manager who says that he knows the investment environment will be inflationary but makes no distinction between periods of accelerating and decelerating inflation. It is not enough to recognize that inflation will never end and to invest on that basis. Your money manager must go much further than that. He must have a method for picking the points when inflation will speed up and when it will slow down. Find out what that method is and make sure you understand it.

MONEY MANAGEMENT QUESTION No. 4

How does your organization time its purchases and sales of various assets? There may be an investment genius hidden in a major bank's trust department somewhere in the country who really knows how to *Beat Inflation*. But all he may be able to do is chalk up paper profits on a mythical portfolio somewhere in his head. He is probably operating under institutional restraints that prevent him from timing his investment decisions correctly. Even if your prospective investment manager answers Questions 1 to 3 to your liking he still may not be the man for you. Institutions frequently impose restraints on individuals that prevent them from quickly changing their portfolios when economic conditions change. This is part of the syndrome that makes all portfolio managers alike, so that they buy the same stocks and bonds as everybody else. The *Beat Inflation* money manager must have the flexibility to take advantage of changes in the inflation rate through making major changes in his portfolio very quickly. Therefore he must have an early warning system for spotting changes in the inflation rate and complete freedom to move when he gets his signal. Find out what restraints institutions put on their money managers.

MONEY MANAGEMENT QUESTION NO. 5

Will the investment manager who runs your portfolio have the freedom to invest in other countries? When an investment manager spots changes in the inflation rate, he has enough asset options open to him so that he can make money for you even if he confines his investments to one country. But there are times when the most visible and surest *Beat Inflation* plays are abroad. Accordingly, an investment manager who can invest in all countries or all currencies can be successful more easily than one who can't. An investment adviser who couldn't take advantage of the shift in the Japanese yen in 1973–74 was behind the eight ball as compared to anybody who could. Clearly, the more choices an investment adviser has open to him, the better off you'll be.

The fatal mistake in dealing with investment managers is to be overwhelmed by them and their surroundings. The stock market has been sick since 1968 even though, and maybe because, it has been dominated by professional investment managers. If there is one man who deserves the title "Father of Security Analysis" it is Benjamin Graham, the senior author of *Security Analysis*. The first edition of this book appeared in 1934.

Here is what he said in 1974 about the performance of the people he and his students have trained:

> . . . the effect of large-scale participation by institutions in the equity market, and the work of innumerable financial analysts striving to establish proper valuation for all sorts, should be to stabilize stock-market movements, i.e., in theory at least, to dampen the unjustified fluctuation in stock prices. I must confess, however, that I have seen no such result flowing from the preponderant position of the institutions in market activity. The amplitude of price fluctuations has, if anything, been wider than before the institutions came into the market on a grand scale. What can be the reason? The

only one I can give is that the institutions and their financial analysts have not shown any more prudence and vision than the general public; they seem to have succumbed to the same siren songs—expressed chiefly in the cult of "performance." . . . (This leads me to ask whether some day soon we shall see some legal problems for certain banking institutions growing out of their accountability for the results of *trust* investments made from 1968 to 1973 that failed to meet the strict judicial requirements of the prudent man rule.)

This is a strong statement, coming from Mr. Prudence himself. It should tell you that you cannot assume that anyone will automatically do a good job in managing your money. Even if the money is in somebody else's hands, constant monitoring of his performance is crucial.

12

Building a
Beat Inflation Portfolio

All the building blocks are now in place. The *Beat Inflation* investor is now ready to assemble a portfolio of bonds, cash, commodities, stocks and currencies that will profit from inflation. The principles have been spelled out in the various chapters concerning each of the assets. Here is a systematic way for allowing you to bet your money on these principles.

Our approach is radical and new. It asks the typical prudent American to consider an investment strategy that in the noninflationary world that existed prior to 1965 would have been considered strictly for the far-outs in the investment community. However, it is the only way that the ordinary American can make his family's wealth grow in a world of high and volatile inflation.

Before you embark full speed ahead in developing a *Beat Inflation* portfolio you have got to get yourself into a position to benefit from the *Beat Inflation* rules. This requires two steps. Painful as it may be, it is smart to get rid of the cats and dogs in your portfolio. If you are like many other Americans, you now hold some bombed-out mutual funds, some series E or H government bonds, plus a melange of stocks that you wonder why you ever bought. Get rid of them. The speed with which you do this will partly depend upon tax considerations. There is a limit to the amount of capital losses that can be used to offset your current income. However, tax considerations should not play a major role. Once you get rid of those cats and dogs, you will be born into a new investment life. And on your first day of that life you should put your money into short-term money market instruments, such as Treasury bills, money market funds or high-grade commercial paper if you realize at least $25,000 from the sale of your investment portfolio.

The next thing to do is to put yourself into a position to borrow as much as you can as quickly as you can. This doesn't mean that you have to borrow the money right away. It does, however, mean to cultivate your local banker and build up whatever lines of credit you can for use when you need to borrow.

Once you have completed these steps, you are ready to set out on the *Beat Inflation* path. You are liquid and in a position to use leverage. Getting liquid and in a position to use leverage by obtaining lines of credit is like making sound opening moves in a chess game. You are ready to pounce on every opportunity and to take advantage of other people's mistakes. The *Beat Inflation* investor knows that those mistakes occur when the price of an asset does not fully reflect the inflation that the *Beat Inflation* investor expects. As you follow the *Beat Inflation* strategy you will be moving into and out of this liquid position. But never give up liquidity unless the odds that a play will work are very high.

One rule of thumb that was followed by "successful" money managers in the 1950s and early 1960s was to stay fully invested. Many people still suffer from this hangover. But our rule of thumb is exactly the opposite—stay liquid, fully liquid, unless you have a very strong reason for doing otherwise. Remember that there is no asset for all seasons and being frozen into the wrong asset for a particular season will cost you dearly.

In a world of high and volatile inflation, a fully liquid portfolio is not so bad a place to be. Short-term interest rates will move up and down with the inflation rate, and therefore your wealth and income will in general keep pace with inflation. There will be periods in which interest rates will move down before the inflation rate moves down and periods when interest rates move up after the inflation rate moves up. But on average an investor who keeps his assets in a fully liquid portfolio—consisting of money market instruments—will do better than most investors.

Moreover, the relationship between swings in the price level and swings in interest rates should be even tighter in the future than in the past. There have been periods when short-term rates and inflation did not march in exact step. This was because the money illusion was hard at work. When inflation soared ahead, interest sometimes moved up much more slowly because lenders and borrowers felt that the rate of price increase would soon fall back to its old level. But the money illusion is nearly dead, and people are getting harder to fool about the future rate of inflation.

If you want to *Beat Inflation* rather than just keep up with it, you must be prepared to get out of a fully liquid position at the right moment. And that moment comes when your assessment of the future inflation rate differs markedly from what the average assessment is as revealed by interest rates and prices of all other assets. The key to the *Beat Inflation* strategy is therefore to decide where the economy is with respect to the inflation cycle.

In Chapter 2, on the inflation cycle, we argued that changes in the money-supply growth rate were the single most important factor causing changes in the inflation rate. Therefore, the key to successful investment is understanding what is happening to the money supply and what it will do to the inflation rate and therefore to interest rates, stock prices, commodity prices, and foreign exchange rates. Keeping track of the money supply is a difficult task. But fortunately there will be plenty of help available.

The key source of data is a maverick regional member of the Federal Reserve system, the Federal Reserve Bank of St. Louis. Over the years this bank had led the way in compiling data on monetary growth rates, not only in the United States but around the world. A letter or postcard addressed to the Federal Reserve Bank of St. Louis, P.O. Box 442, St. Louis, Missouri 63166, will bring you a mountain of data organized in a way that will tell you everything you need to know about domestic and world money-supply growth rates. Furthermore, it all comes free.

When you write your postcard ask for the following publications:

Monetary Trends comes to you monthly and will help you determine the trend rate of monetary growth as well as the current rate. Figure 19 is lifted bodily from the January 1975 issue of *Monetary Trends*. The chart shows that between January 1972 and December 1974 the money supply grew at a compound annual rate of 6½ percent. This is a long enough period to get an estimate of the trend rate of monetary growth. Remember that the rate of monetary growth that prevails for about three years is the trend rate of monetary growth.

But, as always, the most important question for the *Beat Inflation* investor is whether the inflation rate is about to accelerate or decelerate. And here *Monetary Trends* also proves invaluable. Figure 19 shows, for example, that the rate of monetary growth dropped off sharply in the second half of 1974. Between June 1974 and December 1974 the money supply grew at a 2.8 percent compounded annual rate. This should have served as a warning to the *Beat Inflation* investor that in the future inflation would decelerate. Furthermore, remember the other factor that was working toward a deceleration of the inflation rate in late 1974 and early

Figure 19
MONEY STOCK

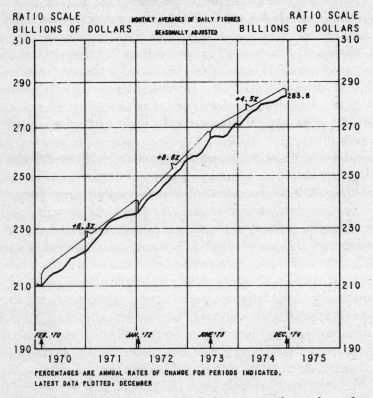

RATIO SCALE   MONTHLY AVERAGES OF DAILY FIGURES   RATIO SCALE
BILLIONS OF DOLLARS   SEASONALLY ADJUSTED   BILLIONS OF DOLLARS

PERCENTAGES ARE ANNUAL RATES OF CHANGE FOR PERIODS INDICATED.
LATEST DATA PLOTTED: DECEMBER

1975. In Chapter 2 we argued that a number of random events pushed the inflation rate higher in 1973 and 1974 than the rate of monetary growth itself would have suggested, and that once these factors were removed inflation would move down on this ground alone.

U. S. *Financial Data* tells you what is happening to the U.S. monetary growth rate every week. It therefore can be used as a basis for updating you on monetary growth between issues of *Monetary Trends*. It also provides a convenient weekly source on both short-term and long-term interest rates.

The weekly data are useful and should be kept readily at hand. But beware of reading too much into week-to-week movements in the money supply. These data jump around quite a bit on a week-to-week basis and are often subject to substantial revisions.

Rates of Change in Economic Data for Ten Industrial Countries comes out quarterly and gives you information on the monetary growth rates in each country as well as the inflation rate and the growth in output. It will enable you to continuously update data on monetary growth rates in other countries.*

These publications are the minimum tool kit for the *Beat Inflation* investor. You probably also ought to get the St. Louis Federal Reserve to send you its *Review,* which often contains articles on how money impacts inflation, interest rates and asset prices around the world. It might also be helpful to get from them a publication entitled *Annual U.S. Economic Data,* which will give data going back some twenty years on money supply, prices and output. This will enable you to put everything into long historical perspective—long enough to pick out changes in the trend rate of inflation and to see how the inflation cycle has behaved in the past.

Once you get these publications under your belt you are a serious *Beat Inflation* investor. There are a few things that you know extremely well, so well in fact, that if somebody woke you up at night and asked the questions below, you could spit out the answers before you were really awake.

What is the trend rate of monetary growth? Right now the St. Louis Federal Reserve says that it is about 6½ percent per year. This is the monetary growth rate that prevailed between January 1972 and the end of 1974.

* You may also want to receive our periodically issued *Beat Inflation Supplement,* providing our current analysis of the inflation cycle and the suitability of various assets for the stage that lies ahead. To receive this *Supplement,* simply fill in the order card in the front of this book, or write directly, enclosing your check or money order for $2.95 to Simon and Schuster, 630 Fifth Avenue, New York, New York 10020.

What is the trend rate of inflation? From Chapter 2 you know that the trend rate of inflation is about one percentage point below the trend rate of money growth. Therefore, your answer is that the trend rate of inflation is about 5½ percent.

What is the current rate of monetary growth? This will be the monetary growth rate over the most recent twelve months. On January 1, 1975, this rate was 4.6 percent. If this monetary growth rate is below the trend rate of monetary growth, you must be prepared for a deceleration phase of the inflation cycle. On January 1, 1975, the most recent monetary growth rate was below the trend rate of monetary growth. If the current monetary growth rate is above the trend rate, then you must be alert to the possibility of an accelerating phase of the inflation cycle.

What is the current rate of price increase? To find out what the current rate of inflation is, another Federal Reserve Bank of St. Louis publication, the monthly *National Economic Trends,* will prove useful. A chart in the January 1975 issue of this publication shows that as the U.S. economy moved into 1975, the current rate of inflation was 12.6 percent. Remembering that the trend rate of inflation is about 1 percent below the trend rate of monetary growth, and that as the economy moved into 1975 the trend of monetary growth was 6½ percent, it was clear that the current rate of inflation was running well ahead of the trend rate of inflation and that a period of decelerating inflation lay ahead.

Having the answers to these questions readily at hand would have allowed the investor to steer a profitable course during the inflation cycles that have occurred since the Vietnam War. Late 1974 was a classic period in which getting answers to these questions would have convinced the *Beat Inflation* investor that the odds overwhelmingly favored the onset of a decelerating phase of the inflation cycle. The money-supply growth rate was running well below the trend of monetary growth and the current inflation rate was running way above the trend rate of inflation. This was the perfect time to change from liquidity to an aggressive posture to take advantage of decelerating inflation.

Moreover, the assets that would benefit from a deceleration in the rate of inflation were selling at knockdown prices. Long-term interest rates were at record highs and less than first quality bonds were selling at prices that more than reflected the tough times that were looming ahead.

The *Beat Inflation* investor would have put some of his chips on bonds. The other great investment at this phase of deceleration was common stocks. The Dow Jones Industrial Average had hit a twelve-year low on December 6, 1974. And as in the case of bonds, the divergence between what the general public believed would happen to inflation and what the *Beat Inflation* investor believed would happen was as wide as the Pacific Ocean. Clearly the beginning of 1975 was the time to build a portfolio of stocks and bonds.

The obverse occurred in 1972. Watergate was not the only thing that Richard M. Nixon did to insure victory over McGovern. The government also ran huge deficits that were accompanied by big increases in the money supply—8.3 percent from December, 1971 to December, 1972. Moreover, foreign governments were also jacking up their money supplies. A surge in inflation was foreordained. That was a time to make investments for accelerating inflation: commodities, short-term money market instruments, stock and bond short sales. Anyone who did this in late 1972 really *Beat Inflation*.

The reported money supply usually gives reliable investment signals as it did in 1972 and 1974. But be a mite careful. The money supply figures reported by the Federal Reserve are not engraved in stone but rather are subject to major revisions. These revisions are made infrequently and therefore the reported money supply numbers can give off false signals. The monetary growth rate decelerated in 1973, for example, but not by as much as originally reported. At the end of 1973, the monetary growth rate was officially reported at 5 per cent from December 1972 to December 1973. After revision, however, it turned out that money actually grew by 5.7 percent.

There are many other instances of a large divergence between the originally reported monetary growth rate and the final revision. Therefore, the *Beat Inflation* investor must have some check on what the money growth rate figures themselves are showing. Fortunately, the Federal Reserve Bank of St. Louis itself provides such a check. In its basic publication, *Monetary Trends*, growth rates are presented on the monetary base, the raw material out of which money is created.

The relationship between the money supply and the monetary base is complex. Ordinarily, however, their growth rates are within 1 percent of each other. Because the monetary base is not subject to large and frequent revision, its movements provide a check for movements in the money supply. If the money-supply growth rates differ from the monetary-base growth rate by more than 1 percent, be careful. The money-supply figure should be suspect—don't make your investment decision on that money-supply number itself. Adjust the money-supply figure upward or downward to reflect what is going on with the monetary base: upward if the monetary base is rising faster than the money supply, downward if the monetary base is rising more slowly. If the signals are still clear after this is done, go ahead and make the investment decision that your reading of the monetary situation suggests.

Once the *Beat Inflation* investor gets a grip on the inflation rate he expects, he faces the problem of adapting his portfolio. The general rule is now simple and apparent: You are always heavily invested in those instruments whose prices are out of line with your view of the inflation prospects. In a world of high and volatile inflation, this can occur at any time. But there are times when under- and overvaluation are

more likely than others. Under-or-over valuation is likely to
be greatest when the monetary growth cycle forecasts a turn
in the inflation cycle that has not yet actually occurred. This
is because the general market will not see the impending
turn in the inflation rate. Consequently, asset prices will be
determined based on views of the inflation rate that are
doomed to be incorrect.

The longer the accelerating phase or the decelerating
phase of an inflation cycle remains in force, the more likely
it is that other investors will be acting in a way to change
asset prices to conform with the *Beat Inflation* investor's
view. This suggests that the rewards are great for those
who can move quickly at turning points and stick to their
guns through a couple of weeks or months of adverse experience.

We are now in a position to summarize.

Decelerations in the rate of growth of the money supply
give way to accelerations when the Federal Reserve begins
to shift its concern from fighting inflation to worrying about
falling output and rising unemployment. The swing toward
faster monetary growth may well occur before inflation
shows signs of a material de-escalation. This is because the
men who run the Federal Reserve know, just as you do, that
it takes time for faster monetary growth to affect the economy. Typically, faster monetary growth leads to higher output and employment within six months, but it takes at least
eighteen months for it to show up in more inflation.

Stocks are ideal when monetary growth is in the initial
stages of accelerating and inflation is still decelerating. The
Graham-Dodd equation will look super. A fall in interest
rates has a tonic effect on stock prices because it reduces
the attractiveness of alternative forms of investment. Interest
rates fall just as the money growth rate is turning around,
not only because the increase in money nudges them down
but also because inflation will be decelerating and price

expectations will be reduced. Moreover, although profits will decline, security analysts will be saying that "the quality" of profits is improving as so-called inventory profits get smaller. In addition, since the re-acceleration in the monetary growth rate will stimulate output, the profits performance of most companies will be much better than people expected. Clearly when you anticipate that the monetary growth rate will turn around, it is an ideal time to buy stocks.

It is also an ideal time to buy bonds. The key to a good performance by bonds is decelerating inflation, which will continue for some time even after the monetary growth rate turns around. With decelerating inflation, price expectations are lowered and long-term interest rates come down some. Therefore bond prices will normally go up, even though monetary growth has already turned around.

Moving through the inflation cycle, the next question that the *Beat Inflation* investor faces is when to start thinking about switching out of stocks and bonds and into other assets. The signals for getting out of bonds and stocks will be most clearly visible in the bond market. But the bond market signal should also be used for the stock market. Be prepared to move out of bonds and stocks when the inflation premium built into bond yields falls down to the trend rate of inflation that is imbedded in your mind as well as in the trend rate of monetary growth. Although bond yields may fall further, the risk/reward ratio of investing in them no longer warrants including bonds in your *Beat Inflation* portfolio. The same will be true of stocks. Since all financial markets march to the same drummer, when the inflation premium in bonds is equal to the trend rate of inflation the inflation premium in stocks will probably also equal the trend rate of inflation. Like bonds, stocks may continue to rise beyond this point, but again like bonds, the risk/reward ratio to holding them begins to rise.

When the inflation rate drops back down to the trend rate,

chances are that the economy will start giving off signals that suggest that the time has come to pull in your horns on stocks and bonds. Unemployment will probably stop rising and the amount of general slack in the economy will stop growing. Since money has been growing fast for quite a while, many investors will begin to expect the inflation rate to turn around.

The point at which interest rates reflect the trend of inflation that you believe will persist is the time to begin getting out of stocks and bonds. It is also the time to start thinking about commodities—gold, as well as real estate and short-term liquid assets. Accelerating inflation is around the corner.

Remember that when monetary growth first turns upward it results in higher employment and higher output, while inflation continues to decelerate for a while. It is during this period that stocks and bonds are the great play. It is after inflation begins to accelerate that hard assets are the great play. Remember what is happening in the economy. Output has responded to the turn in monetary policy with a lag of three to six months. After output and employment expand, the pressures on prices increase and the economy moves into the early stages of accelerating inflation. This is the season for commodities, including gold. But hard assets are to be played very carefully—only under the conditions that make you sure their price embodies a far different inflation rate than you yourself think is likely.

The time when hard assets become super-dangerous to hold is when the Federal Reserve is about to step on the monetary brakes as it did in the first half of 1973 and again in the second half of 1974. At this point, the economy will be pushing capacity to the limit, inventory accumulation will be excessive and there will be a general shortage mentality. Once the Federal Reserve steps on the brakes a reduction in the rate of monetary growth is not far away. This is a good

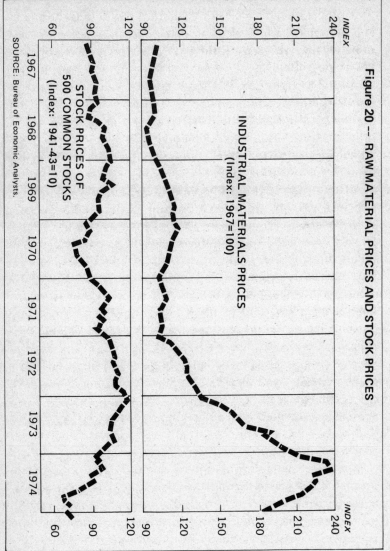

Figure 20 -- RAW MATERIAL PRICES AND STOCK PRICES

INDUSTRIAL MATERIALS PRICES
(Index: 1967=100)

STOCK PRICES OF
500 COMMON STOCKS
(Index: 1941-43=10)

SOURCE: Bureau of Economic Analysts.

point at which to get liquid, because nothing very good is going to happen for a while. The initial stages of tight money will play hell with stock and bond prices and although commodities may rise for a little while their prices have become very vulnerable. But the *Beat Inflation* investor can be very comfortable indeed. Short-term interest rates on securities where there is minimal chance of capital loss will be sky high. The *Beat Inflation* investor can get his portfolio into a fully liquid position in anticipation of a swing from monetary deceleration to monetary acceleration sometime in the future.

All this sounds relatively simple, and for a good reason. It is relatively simple. Prior to casting off the shadow of Poor Richard, the investment scene in a world of high and variable inflation seemed like a jumbled mess to the authors themselves. But once we realized that inflation would never end, but that there would be a steady progression of inflation cycles, we were able to formulate a way of looking at investment vehicles in which all the component parts fell into place. A major tenet—perhaps *the* major tenet—of the *Beat Inflation* approach is that the prices of hard assets such as gold and commodities rise when the prices of financial assets such as stocks and bonds fall, and vice versa. Figure 20 shows the inverse relationship between the prices of the commodities included in the Bureau of Labor Statistics Index of Industrial Materials Prices and the Standard and Poor's 500 Stock Index. It shows that when commodity prices are rising, stock prices are falling and that when commodity prices are falling, stock prices are rising. That is the way it has been since the birth of the inflation cycle and that is the way it will continue.

APPENDIX

If We Have
Wage and Price Controls

On-again off-again price and wage controls will be a fact of life in a world of high and volatile inflation. However, controls are likely to be imposed at predictable times, go through predictable episodes of tightening and loosening and have predictable effects on asset prices. Accordingly, the *Beat Inflation* investor need never be victimized by controls; instead, he can adopt strategies that make them work to his advantage.

An atmosphere in which controls are present or latent will not fundamentally change the investment strategy outlined in the previous chapters. Controls will not put an end to the inflation cycle; in fact they will help cause it to continue. Nor will they put an end to the transfers of income and wealth that inflation brings.

WHEN THE GOVERNMENT LOOKS TO CONTROLS

Decisions of whether or not to put on controls are best considered as political decisions. In the policy makers' calculus, controls have certain obvious advantages and disadvantages. On the plus side, they allow the White House to project an executive image when there is a public outcry to "do something about inflation." In addition they shift the focus of attention away from the real culprits of inflation, the government's own agencies—the Federal Reserve and the Treasury—toward the private sector and the struggle between business and labor to maintain their income shares.

The public relations value of this is difficult to overestimate. It has to be a great relief to the White House when Walter Cronkite talks about the leaders in business or labor and the confrontations they create against the "public interest" when they try to raise prices and wages. The government's role then shows up as the protector of the "public interest" rather than culprit in the inflation process. Electronic journalism is perfectly suited to this shift in focus. It has a horrendous time depicting the complex processes by which the Federal Reserve creates inflation, but a very easy time showing its viewers conflict between, say, management and labor or consumers and supermarkets. And in these conflicts the government always looks good. It is obvious that government officials have no selfish interest in these conflicts. Therefore they come out as the defenders of the "public interest" and as the protectors against selfish business and labor leaders. This is a role in which government officials wear white hats and come on like Marshal Dillon.

On the minus side, this strong executive image suffers from the same problem that afflicts most TV shows and with far more devastating consequences. It does not reflect reality. On TV, Marshal Dillon always ends up by vanquishing the villain; in the real world, inflation always ends up by vanquishing controls.

The problem with image building is that it's just that. It doesn't deal with the fundamental problem of the causes of inflation and how to eliminate them. It deals instead with symptoms of inflation. Rising prices and wages do not cause inflation. As the *Beat Inflation* investor knows, the inflation cycle is produced by what happens to monetary and fiscal policy.

Tight wage and price controls have a very short life in the Western democracies. The reason is simply that the money-supply growth rate is accelerating on average; therefore, based on the fundamentals, inflation is accelerating more than it is decelerating. And when inflation accelerates it always ends up by blowing up the controls programs. When money growth accelerates so does the demand for goods and services, and price pressures begin to mount. If controls prevent prices from rising, the conflicts over competing income shares get intense and arguments over whose ox is gored become militant. Controls also tend to make the inflationary pressures even worse than they otherwise would be. They discourage production and encourage businessmen and labor to devote a substantial portion of time to trying to outwit controls. Businessmen usually find ways around controls, which is fortunate for the functioning of the economy, but there are much more productive uses of their time— which is one reason why controls tend to reduce productivity.

The economies of Western democracies are strewn with dead and wounded controls programs. In fact, just prior to President Nixon's decision to implement his new economic program on August 15, 1971, a study commissioned and paid for by his own Council of Economic Advisers detailed the abysmal performance of controls in Western Europe. But just as this study didn't stop President Nixon from implementing controls, further evidence of their failure, including that of Nixon's program itself, will not stop future governments from imposing them. Therefore, the *Beat Inflation* investor must be able to anticipate controls and work them into his investment strategy.

How Controls Fit Into the Inflation Cycle

As a general rule, the *Beat Inflation* investor can expect controls when the public-relations pluses exceed the fundamental economic minuses. The balance is likely to be in favor of controls when the economy is in the decelerating phase of the inflation cycle. The notion that the government is most likely to impose controls when inflation is fated to decelerate anyway may seem paradoxical. And on economic grounds it is paradoxical. But on political and public-relations grounds it makes perfect sense.

In the decelerating phase of the inflation cycle, unemployment will be rising, output will be falling and inflation will be showing signs of coming down. At the same time television will be showing lots of conflict. Strike activity will be on the rise. This is a time when the President's political advisers will tell him he must project an executive image. And it is also a time when his economic advisers will tell him that controls would give the appearance of working. Demand has been wrung out by tight money, and there is considerable slack in the economy. Shortsighted as this view may be, the President may feel that he will look good for at least six months, and considering lags involved, controls may help carry him through an election.

An illustration of this process is provided by what happened with President Nixon's new economic policy that was instituted in August 1971. This was a period of decelerating inflation. Inflation had peaked out in 1970 and was on its way down during 1971. However, the unemployment rate was still hanging high, output was expanding slowly and inflation was coming down in niggardly little steps. In addition, a Presidential election was coming up in 1972. Here in the same pot were all the necessary ingredients: political need, and economic possibility. Controls were thus instituted and inflation continued to decelerate. At last Walter Cronkite and Dan Rather could say something nice about the President. Here was a program. The President was indeed doing something about inflation.

Nor did the benefits end there. With controls in place, the Federal Reserve could be even more comfortable in reaccelerating monetary growth. The decelerating phase of the inflation cycle is the "right" time to institute controls and jack up money growth. Thus Nixon could have executive image with controls, rising employment as he moved toward the 1972 election, and deferral until after November to pay the piper on inflation. This game was played with a vengeance during the Watergate year of 1972. It may not be played with such vengeance again, but the probability that it will be played in some form must enter the calculations of the *Beat Inflation* investor. For, while the players will be chastened, the same political calculus will exist and the answer will be the same. The leads and lags will not disappear and politicians still prefer jam today to jam tomorrow. Therefore, the *Beat Inflation* investor should expect controls during periods of decelerating inflation, particularly 12 to 18 months before a Presidential election.

He should expect the removal of controls when the previous monetary expansion shows up in tight labor markets, high rates of factory capacity utilization and prevalent shortages in key commodities. Under these conditions the political minuses begin to outweigh the political pluses. In all the industrial democracies, labor unions in particular have the ability to blow the executive image of Presidents and prime ministers to smithereens. The fact is that any major labor confederation such as the AFL–CIO can pull enough workers out of plants to impose hefty wage settlements that exceed whatever guidelines may be in effect. Caving in in the face of labor threats has ended the career of many European politicians up to and including General de Gaulle.

In the United States controls have come off well before the occurrence of major confrontations. U.S. politicians have wisely preferred switching to fighting. And usually when the switch comes, the crowd, which previously had been clamoring for controls, cheers. Businessmen are sick of shortages, distortions and dealing with the bureaucrats who administer the controls. And although consumer interest groups are still concerned with prices they sense that there is something wrong with the distribution system. Labor sees some uncontrolled prices, like food and bank interest rates, rising, and would like to jump on the bandwagon. Everybody begins criticizing the controls, even the controllers themselves, and with no political pluses and large economic minuses the controls program falls by the wayside.

To summarize, the moral of this political analysis for the *Beat Inflation* investor is this: Relatively tight controls are likely to be a phenomenon of decelerating inflation, loose controls or no controls at all a phenomenon of accelerating inflation. This may seem to be a paradox, but this is the way it has been all around the world, and it is likely to continue this way.

WHAT CONTROLS DO AND WHAT THEY DON'T DO

The *Beat Inflation* investor knows that the ups and downs of the inflation cycle are determined by the swings in the monetary growth rate. Therefore the rule of thumb for the *Beat Inflation* investor with respect to controls is: Don't expect them to do what their proponents claim they will do. Nevertheless, controls do have some impact. And, even more important, they will often create investment opportunities because they will at times cause divergences between what the *Beat Inflation* investor will expect to happen to prices and what everybody else will expect to happen to prices.

Here are three effects that the *Beat Inflation* investor can expect controls to have.

1. *Controls are likely to intensify the inflation cycle.* There are many reasons why this is so. The most important is their impact on the psychology of the Board of Governors of the Federal Reserve System. Remember that controls tend to be put into effect in the decelerating phase of the inflation cycle and that a drop in the inflation rate comes about only after production has weakened and unemployment has risen. These of course are the conditions under which policy makers switch their goals from fighting inflation to combating recession and unemployment. When they switch, policy makers have in the back of their minds the idea that expansive monetary policy will eventually lead to a reacceleration in the inflation rate. But with controls in place, the Governors, if history is a guide, feel emboldened to swing to sharply higher monetary growth. Depending on how well they understand economics, they may or may not feel that controls will work. However, being good bureaucrats, they know that they would have to take the blame for deepening unemployment if they sat on their hands. But they would be able to shunt the responsibility for the reaccelerating of inflation to the dropping of controls.

It is worth observing that world central bankers tend to favor controls because they create confusion over the real causes of inflation. In this context it is highly significant to note that Federal Reserve Board Chairman Arthur F. Burns was an opponent of controls when in private practice at the National Bureau of Economic Research. But he became a strong proponent when he took over the leadership of the Federal Reserve's bureaucracy.

Since the monetary acceleration that occurs during a recession tends to be greater when controls are in place than in their absence, the business cycle upswing that follows the recessionary period is more likely to get out of hand. With the strong monetary stimulus that can be applied behind the mask of controls, extreme inflationary pressures will reappear with a vengeance. As a consequence, on-again off-again controls are one reason why the trend rate of inflation will be increasing in the long run. At the same time, the inflation cycle itself is likely to be more volatile.

The moral of this story for the investor is this: When and if controls come, don't be fooled into thinking they will stop inflation. Indeed, the lessons of history suggest that a *Beat Inflation* strategy will be more vital than ever. In fact, keep watching for public outcries to remove controls, for these will be another sign that controls will be coming off and inflation will accelerate rapidly.

2. *Controls distort the reported price index numbers, particularly at the wholesale level.* There is a widely accepted body of evidence that shows that businessmen behave the way you would expect them to behave. When the political and economic atmosphere threatens controls, companies use every possible opportunity to jack up their list prices. They may not always want or be able to sell at these prices, but having high published prices clearly gives them room to maneuver on the upside when and if tight controls are imposed. It so happens that the price indexes, particularly the wholesale price index, are primarily based on list prices rather than "transaction" or "contract" prices—the prices at which goods actually change hands. As a consequence, controls make the trend of the price indexes, especially the wholesale price index, show more inflation than it would in the absence of controls. The businessman who has his stockholders' interest, as well as his own job security, at heart will make his price concessions in a way that keeps list prices intact. There are many methods of shading prices—absorbing transportation costs, giving bigger quantity discounts, and doing whatever else can be done to satisfy the customer.

3. *Controls create distortions in the economy, reducing*

productivity growth and increasing long-term inflationary pressures. The minute controls go on, a large number of people inevitably get involved in a rather unproductive game. The administrators of the program must concentrate on enforcing the rules and interpreting the regulations, which can be tough. The controlees must get involved in filling out forms, learning the regulations and devising ways to get around controls. These endeavors involve highly intelligent people in an essentially wasteful task. This in itself is inflationary—these workers are paid salaries and they produce nothing.

But the real problems come in when controls actually "work." The history of periods of controls are replete with examples of horrendous problems of production bottlenecks and slowdowns caused by controls. Examples of this are numerous. When price controls were imposed on copper and lumber, and so on, in 1972 and 1973, severe shortages occurred in the United States because the domestic price was held below the world price and a huge share of output was exported. Any time prices are held below what supply-and-demand forces dictate, a mess ensues. And when messes cluster, output shrinks and inflationary pressures increase.

In summary, controls increase the trend rate of inflation, intensify the inflation cycle, distort the price indexes and reduce productivity growth and output. In short, they do far more harm than good. What they don't do is reduce inflation or make it go away. The problem for the *Beat Inflation* investor is to minimize the harm that they do to his income and wealth. Fortunately there are a number of investment rules that can allow the investor to make controls work to his advantage.

CONTROLS RULE NO. 1

The imposition of controls will give the *Beat Inflation* investor a second chance at decelerating inflation plays. Since controls are typically imposed after inflation has already begun to decelerate, there is a good chance that market expectations will interpret controls as a further evidence that inflation is really on its way down. Therefore, they are likely to intensify the stock and bond price improvement that is already under way.

The *Beat Inflation* investor can therefore safely hang onto these instruments longer than he may otherwise have. In effect, this would represent a windfall gain. If Dan Rather and Walter Cronkite really have people convinced that controls will work, then the market's expectation of inflation is likely to be knocked down below the trend rate. There could therefore be a sharp improvement in the total return from holding decelerating-phase investment vehicles. If you play this kind of game, it is safer to be in bonds or intermediate securities rather than stocks. Remember the distortions and confusion created by controls. Uncertainty doesn't do the Graham and Dodd equation any good. In addition, controls can be highly discriminatory, and security analysts, like everybody else, will have great difficulty in figuring out how. Thus, it is easy to get sandbagged in the wrong stock or stock group.

Bonds, you will remember, are the purest play on inflation expectations. An improvement in the public's perception of inflation will do wonders for bond prices and the total return to the bond investor.

CONTROLS RULE NO. 2

A controls-induced decelerating inflation play should be made carefully and terminated relatively promptly. It won't take long for the fact that controls have little effect on the trend rate of inflation to assert itself in the marketplace. Thus, the decline in interest rates brought on by controls is apt to take on a V-shape rather quickly. The *Beat Inflation* investor should remember the fundamental futility of controls and not get carried away.

CONTROLS RULE NO. 3

When controls come off, the *Beat Inflation* investor will get a second chance at accelerating-inflation plays. Since controls typically come off after monetary policy has become superexpansive and all seeds for a burst of inflation have been planted, their removal can be expected to boost commodity prices sharply. It is also likely that long-term price expectations will shoot up and that bond prices will drop. In addition, the Graham and Dodd equation will again produce confusing results and lower stock prices, although basic raw-material-producing companies may escape for a time. Obviously commodity plays can and will look good. In fact, the actual rate of inflation will shoot above the trend rate for a time. This improves the chances of making money on accelerating-inflation plays such as commodities.

CONTROLS RULE NO. 4

A controls-induced accelerating-inflation play should be made carefully, but it need not be terminated as promptly as the controls-induced decelerating-inflation play. After controls are taken off, prices are likely to really shoot up and continue rising for some time. The Federal Reserve will gradually shift its policy goal toward price stability but it is likely to overstay on the expansionary side because it is more worried about unemployment than it is about inflation. Remember the inflationary bias in policy and the money illusion. It will take more and more stimulus to get the unemployment rate to move down.

Following these rules, the *Beat Inflation* investor should be able to take controls in stride. He knows that controls will end neither inflation nor the inflation cycle but will intensify both.

GLOSSARY

It is especially incumbent on the authors of a book of practical advice to spell out clearly what they mean. We therefore provide this glossary in the spirit of the famous philosopher Alfred North Whitehead, who once said, "A definition a day keeps the charlatan away." Many of the terms you need to know to talk the language of investment and money management are in this list. There are two kinds of entries. The words in *italics* are part of the standard language of investing. These are the kinds of words you need to know to talk to your broker or to read the financial press quickly.

The words listed in SMALL CAPITALS are some of the special terms that we have used in developing an investment strategy particularly suited to a world of high and volatile inflation. They form a partial lexicon of inflation. The beginning investor will probably wish to skim all the definitions. The more experienced investor can safely take the SMALL CAPITAL route.

Balance Sheet   Some simple family balance sheets are shown on pages 57–58. Families who *Beat Inflation* think of their financial position mainly in terms of their balance sheets. Company balance sheets are more complicated than family balance sheets. A relatively small company's balance sheet might look like this:

174

Assets		Liabilities and Net Worth	
Current assets		Liabilities	
Cash	$20,000	Current Liabilities	
Inventory	80,000	Accounts Payable	$30,000
Total Current Assets	$100,000	Notes Payable	20,000
Fixed Assets		Total Current Liabilities	$50,000
Equipment	$140,000	Long-Term Liabilities	
Plant	190,000	Bonds	$100,000
Less Accumulated		Total Liabilities	$150,000
Depreciation	30,000	Net Worth	
Total Fixed Assets	$300,000	Preferred Stock	$25,000
Total Assets	$400,000	Common Stock	100,000
		Returned Earnings	125,000
		Total Net Worth	$250,000
		Total	$400,000

The condition of a company can be gauged by balancing assets against liabilities. Assets are what a company owns. Liabilities are what it owes. Its capital or net worth is obtained by subtracting its liabilities from its assets.

High and volatile inflation makes it difficult to evaluate a company by looking at its balance sheet. This is one of the things that has made the years since 1965 so hard on stock prices. Rapidly rising prices raise two basic questions. What will it cost to replace inventories? Are depreciation reserves adequate to replace worn-out and obsolete equipment?

The company whose balance sheet is shown above is a net monetary debtor (see page 58). Its monetary liabilities, both short-term and long-term, equal $150,000. Its monetary assets equal $20,000. This company is a net monetary debtor to the extent of $130,000. From this point of view it is well positioned to benefit from accelerating inflation. But beware—security analysts may get very nervous about this company. It has a lot of inventory and depreciable assets.

Even in the face of double-digit inflation, few companies have explicitly shown what inflation has done and is doing to their earnings and balance sheets. A small telephone company in the

Midwest, Indiana Telephone, however, has been doing this for a number of years. At the beginning of 1975 it was in fact believed to be the only U.S. company that keeps a double set of books and lays them out side by side for shareholders to see. These books consist of conventional accounting statements plus a restatement of accounts to reflect the impact of inflation. Under conventional accounting methods Indiana Telephone showed net earnings of $2.3 million, or $4.55 a share, in 1973. Adjusted for inflation, however, earnings were reported as $1.5 million or $3 a share. The investor can get copies of this company's financial statements by writing to T. Allen Russell, Controller, Indiana Telephone, Seymour, Indiana 47274.

Basis Points   Just as there are ten inklings in a clue, there are 100 basis points in a percentage point. Money market professionals tend to measure interest rate changes in basis points. For example, if the interest rate on 90-day U.S. Treasury Bills rises from 5% to 5¼%, the moneymarketeer would say that the yield has gone up by 25 basis points. The reason for this fine measurement is that day to day changes in yield are small.

Bond   A certificate of debt, pledging to pay a specified sum of money, principal, at a certain date or periodically over the course of a loan. Ordinarily, interest is paid at fixed rates and at specified dates, generally every six months. The fixed interest payment is the most important investment characteristic of a bond, since it means that bond prices fall when market interest rates go up and rise when market interest rates fall. The existence of an inflation cycle means that the biggest investment bang per dollar invested in bonds comes from changes in bond prices rather than from the fixed interest payments. This means that bonds should never again be put in your safe-deposit box and forgotten.

Book Value   The book value of a company is arrived at by subtracting the total value of its liabilities from the total value of its undepreciated assets. It is an accounting measure of value mainly of historical interest. Any relationship between the book value of a company and the market value of its net assets is more likely than not to be a random occurrence. This is particularly true when the inflation cycle is rapidly changing the replacement cost of physical assets and inventories. *Book Value per Share* is simply the total book value of a company divided by the number of shares it has outstanding. Beware of stock recommendations based on the idea that a good buy is a stock selling below book value. The book value of a company tells you nothing about what its stock should sell for.

Cash Equivalent Instruments   Are generally short-term IOUs issued by companies, banks and government. They carry short maturities—one year or less, usually 90 days or less—and are therefore easy to convert into cash at close to their purchase price. *Negotiable Certificates of Deposit* (CDs), *Commercial Paper* and *U.S. Treasury Bills* are the major examples in the U.S. When the *Beat Inflation* strategy tells you to get liquid, invest in these securities or in liquid asset funds composed of these securities.

Commercial Paper   Unsecured promissory notes of well-known companies, including bank holding companies, with strong balance sheets and therefore good credit ratings. Large finance companies, Commercial Credit Corporation, for example, usually sell their paper directly to investors. Corporations usually sell to middlemen, Merrill Lynch or Salomon Brothers, for example, who resell the paper to investors. Ordinarily commercial paper is sold in amounts of at least $25,000. By the end of 1974 there was $49 billion of commercial paper outstanding.

Commodity Contract   A contract agreeing to deliver a fixed amount of a particular commodity, such as soybeans, wheat, copper, on some specified date in the future. Commodity contracts are traded on *Futures Markets*. Before you get into one of these contracts, be very sure you know exactly what you are buying. The major commodity exchanges such as the Chicago Board of Trade and the Chicago Mercantile Exchange have reams of booklets available giving detailed descriptions of the contracts for which they make a market. Your broker has the same kind of information.

Depreciation Allowance or Depreciation   The Internal Revenue Service permits a depreciation allowance to be claimed against any physical earning asset. The allowance is supposed to represent a reasonable estimate of the reduction in its earning power due to wear and tear or to obsolescence. This allowance can be used as a deduction from income before taxes are paid. In theory, the allowance permits a company to accumulate enough money during the earning life of an asset to replace it when it is ready for the scrap heap. When inflation is high and volatile, depreciation allowances tend to be inadequate because the costs of new machinery and plant rise faster than the guidelines for depreciation allowances permitted by the Internal Revenue Service.

Discount Bond   When bonds are first issued they usually are priced to sell close to $1000 per bond or some multiple of $1000. Consequently, the coupon on the bond reflects the current market yield. That is to say, a $1000 bond that pays $90 per year in interest will yield 9%. At any moment in time there will be bonds around that were issued when interest rates were lower than the current market rate. These are discount bonds. Their primary characteristic is that they are now selling at a price well below their issue price because the yields available on newly issued bonds have gone way up. For example, on February 3, 1975, the U.S. Treasury Bonds 3½% of 1998 were selling at around $750 per bond. Since they were issued at about $1000 per bond, they are selling at a large discount. When the *Beat Inflation* strategy tells you to buy bonds, a portfolio of discount bonds will usually outperform a portfolio of similarly rated newly issued bonds.

Dividend   That portion of its earnings that a company decides to pay to its stockholders. Conceptually and usually in practice, the dividend represents a share of the company's profits. When the investor buys a share of common stock he receives no guarantee of the size of the dividend, but preferred stocks do promise a fixed number of dollars per year and sometimes a guarantee that arrears in payments to the preferred stockholders must be met before the holders of common stock receive any dividend at all. The growth stock philosophy of the 1960s was based on the idea that the earnings and dividends of some companies would grow rapidly and steadily. This assumption is unwarranted in a world of high and volatile inflation.

Federal Funds Market   A rapidly developing market where banks with extra reserves (more than the rules of the Federal Reserve require them to hold) lend them to banks with inadequate reserves. The loans are for overnight and typically in multiples of $1000. Private investors cannot invest in federal funds. The most important thing for private investors is not to be fooled by what is happening to the interest rate on federal funds. Many analysts place heavy stress on every twitch in this rate because they believe that all twitches are caused by Federal Reserve policy. Do not believe them. The *Beat Inflation* investor will focus on the monetary growth rate as the indicator of Federal Reserve policy.

FINANCIAL ASSET   A financial asset always has two sides. It is an asset to the individual who buys it. It is a liability to the individual who creates it. A real asset, by contrast, is not somebody's else's liability. Physical assets, like a house and a kilo of gold, are real assets. You may have borrowed to buy them, but the debt you created is your liability and somebody else's financial asset. Any financial asset you own, such as a bond, is somebody else's liability. Technically, stocks are not financial assets. We, however, classify them as financial assets because their prices tend to move up and down at the same time financial asset prices do. Ordinarily, financial assets are good things to get rid of when inflation is about to accelerate and good things to load up on when inflation is about to decelerate.

FINANCIAL LIABILITY   Some evidence of debt stated in dollars or some other monetary unit such as yen or Swiss francs. There is nothing wrong with expanding your liabilities in a period of inflation. A critical element of the *Beat Inflation* strategy is to step up financial liability creation to purchase real assets when you think the inflation rate will speed up. Usually, financial liabilities are expressed in a fixed number of dollars; if you borrow $1000 from the bank, you have to pay back the same number of dollars. There are interest charges, but if the price of the real assets you buy with the money you borrow increases fast enough, the interest charges should be easy to pay off. To *leverage* yourself, there will be periods when you want your financial liabilities to grow very rapidly.

Foreign Exchange Contract   A contract agreeing to deliver a fixed amount of currency on a specified date in the future. It is virtually identical to a *Commodity Contract* except that the item being traded is marks, yen, francs, etc.

Forward   An adjective used to describe the important elements of a deal to be consummated in the future at a price agreed upon in the present. If you guarantee either to buy or sell so many German marks or so many bushels of wheat at a stipulated dollar price on some specified date in the future, then you are dealing in forward marks or forward wheat.

Futures Market   A place where *Commodity Contracts* and *Foreign Exchange Contracts* are traded.

Gold Bug   An investor or investment adviser who places his faith in gold and precious metals alone. The Gold Bug believes that a continual rise in the price of precious metals is inevitable, that they are the only safe investment, and that the destruction of most other forms of wealth, particularly financial assets, is foreordained. By contrast, the *Beat Inflation* investor neither loves nor hates gold; he regards precious metals as just one form of investment particularly suited to accelerating inflation, particularly unsuited to decelerating inflation. The *Beat Inflation* investor holds Gold Bugs in disdain, regarding them as investment primitives.

HARD ASSET   Another name for a REAL ASSET.

Hedging   People hedge because they do not wish to take the risks that occur because prices fluctuate. By the same token they are willing to forego the rewards from guessing right on prices. Most companies that use a lot of raw materials are hedgers. Nestlé's, the chocolate manufacturer, for example, hedges in cocoa. When the company purchases a shipload of cocoa it sells an equal amount in the futures market. That is to say, the company contracts to deliver a shipload of cocoa at a later date for a price that is set on the same day that it receives the shipment. If the price of cocoa falls, the company loses on its cocoa inventories, but gains an equal sum on its future sale because the cocoa called for in the futures contract can be purchased at a lower price. If the price of cocoa rises, the company loses on its future sale but gains on its inventory. In either case, the company has insured itself against the loss caused by price fluctuation.

Hedging is also used in currency markets by companies that know they will need a particular amount of some foreign currency in the future, but do not wish to speculate on a change in its price.

Hyperinflation   Also called runaway inflation or galloping inflation. In the definitive study on hyperinflation, Professor Phillip Cagan of Columbia University and the National Bureau of Economic Research classified an inflation as hyper when prices rose by at least 50 percent per month. Hyperinflation is rare in history and has usually occurred during and after wars. Some classic hyperinflations are described on page 52.

Do not confuse hyperinflation with what will happen in the next decade. Hyperinflation results in a virtually total disruption of economic activity. Inflation will be high and volatile in the next decade but it is unlikely to be hyper.

INFLATION PREMIUM   The inflation premium is that part of an interest rate or a rate of wage gain that is attributable to the expectation of inflation. If there were no inflation there would be no inflation premiums. Interest rates, for example, would be determined by productivity and thrift. The amount that borrowers would be willing to pay would depend only on the degree to which capital increases productivity. The amount that lenders would be willing to supply would depend on attitudes toward thrift. This no-inflation interest rate is relatively stable. Therefore, the big movements in interest rates come from changes in the inflation premium. A discussion of how to measure the inflation premium built into bond yields is contained on pages 78–80.

Inflation   The best definition of inflation is the straightforward one: Inflation means rising prices. You can tell how bad inflation is by looking at what the price indexes compiled by government are doing. The government's indexes of prices are needed to give you a reasonable approximation of what is going on. There are always some prices that are falling and always some that are rising. What is needed is an estimate of what is happening to the price level or prices on average. Broad indexes such as the U.S. Consumer Price Index have their defects, but they are the best gauge around to measure the inflation rate.

Avoid quirky or idiosyncratic definitions of inflation. Some analysts and economists, for example, say that inflation is a rise in quantity of money, or the price of gold or even the rate at which the money supply turns over. Everyone, of course, is entitled to his own definitions. But there is less confusion if they are kept straightforward. To beat it, you must get out of your head and out of your financial planning the idea that inflation is an abnormal state of events.

Leverage   Leverage is a financial arrangement that allows you to increase the potential profit or loss from the use of your own capital. Borrowing is one way of exerting leverage. Suppose, for example, that you buy 100 shares of a stock selling for $50 per share and its price doubles. If you invested your own capital you have doubled your money. But if you borrowed, say, 50 percent of the initial investment, the return on your own $2500 would be 200 percent. That is good leverage.

Liquidity Crisis   A period when there is widespread concern over whether companies and banks will be able to refinance their short-term debt as it comes due. For nonfinancial companies the issue is whether lenders will continue to lend to them. Will the banks permit the company to roll over its short-term borrowings? Will the buyers of commercial paper be willing to take on new commercial paper issues to replace those that are expiring? And can the rollovers be accomplished at interest rates that permit the company to survive? For banks, the issue is whether depositors, including major corporations holding deposits in the form of large CDs, will continue to maintain their balances in the face of adverse rumors. Liquidity crises tend to cluster in the early decelerating phase of the monetary growth cycle, when short-term interest rates hit their peak levels.

LIQUID   A fuzzy word that everybody in the money game uses a lot. The meaning of the word can best be seen in its ordinary uses. As used to describe an investment in the *Beat Inflation* strategy, a highly liquid asset is one that can be turned into cash at something very close to its purchase price. This may be because its maturity is short and its price therefore does not fluctuate very much when interest rates change. It may also be because someone guarantees the repurchase of the security at a fixed price. You can always turn back a series E or H bond to the government and at least get your money quickly. The word liquid is also used to describe the financial condition of companies, banks, or individuals. In the *Beat Inflation* strategy, liquid refers to a financial condition where a large proportion of assets consists of liquid assets. When the *Beat Inflation* rules say "get liquid," they mean load up on liquid assets. There are times when being liquid is a virtue and times when it is a vice. It all depends on the stage of the inflation cycle.

Margin   Margin is the amount that you put up when you use credit to buy securities or to sell them short. When you have a margin account with your broker you can borrow a certain percentage of the purchase price of a security. In the case of common stocks, the maximum percentage is set by the Federal Reserve Board. Margin requirements vary, depending on the asset. They are high for stocks, medium for corporate bonds, and low for U.S. Government bonds and commodities.

Maturity   The date at which a bond, note or loan comes due and must be repaid or rolled over, if bankruptcy has not intervened in the meantime.

MONETARY ASSET (LIABILITY) See FINANCIAL ASSET.

MONEY ILLUSION   If the simple fact that you get more dollars in your pay envelope gives you a psychological high, then you are suffering from the Money Illusion. It arises when someone makes economic decisions without considering the purchasing power of money. The Money Illusion is getting weaker in this country as people keep expecting the inflation rate to be high. This concept plays an important role in the *Beat Inflation* strategy. It is described in detail in pages 22–24.

MONEY SUPPLY   There are at least six valid definitions of the money supply. In *The Beat Inflation Strategy,* we have built our investment theory around the most widely accepted definition, the narrowly defined money supply or M_1. M_1 consists of demand deposits (checking accounts) plus currency and coin held by the non-bank public. The other concepts of the money supply all include M_1 but add some other financial assets. M_2 for example, consists of M_1 plus savings deposits and non-negotiable time certificates at commercial banks. Although each of these other definitions encompasses a somewhat broader view of what constitutes money, they all tend to move in the same direction at the critical turning points. Consequently, most of the time it really doesn't matter which one you focus on so long as you stick to following it and it alone. We have chosen to focus on M_1 because it has performed most consistently in providing the investor with early warnings of prospective swings in the inflation cycle.

Money Market Instruments   See *Cash Equivalent Instruments.*

Negotiable Certificate of Deposit (CD).   A piece of paper indicating that a specific sum of money has been deposited in a commercial bank for a specific period of time, at least thirty days, and at a specific rate of interest. This instrument was invented by First National City Bank in 1961. Since then its use has grown rapidly; at the end of 1974 there were $92.9 billion in CDs outstanding. CDs differ from other bank deposits, since they are negotiable instruments. Dealers make a secondary market for the sale of outstanding issues. The yield on CDs is usually higher than on *U.S. Treasury Bills* because they are perceived as riskier investments. The yield is, however, about the same as on high-grade *Commercial Paper.*

NET MONETARY DEBTOR (CREDITOR)   A Net Monetary Debtor is an individual or a business that has more monetary liabilities than monetary assets. A NET MONETARY CREDITOR has more monetary assets than monetary liabilities. These concepts, vital to the *Beat Inflation* strategy, are discussed in detail on pages 57–58. Also see *Balance Sheet.*

Net Worth   This is the difference between what you owe and what you own, or the difference between your assets and your liabilities. For example, Mr. Net Creditor, whose balance sheet is described on page 57, has a balance sheet that looks like this:

Assets		Liabilities and Net Worth	
Cash	10	Mortgage	5
House	10	Net Worth	15
Total	20	Total	20

His net worth is the value of his assets, $20 (cash $10 plus house $10), minus the value of his mortgage, $5, or $15. The objective of any money management strategy is to increase net worth rather than holdings of stocks, cash, or any other asset.

No Load   Means simply that the sales commission charged for the purchase of an asset is zero. Although high commission rates for mutual funds are gradually on their way out, some still charge as much as 8 to 9 percent. Thus an investor who puts $10,000 in a fund that charges 8 percent will have only $9200 working for him on the first day of his investment. In the days when people believed in a buy-and-hold strategy, these high commission rates did not cause much concern. But in a world of high and volatile inflation they should be ruthlessly avoided. Always look for no-load or low-load investment vehicles. There are good reasons for being a cheapskate about paying sales commissions. First of all, there is no systematic evidence that funds that charge high sales commissions do better than funds that charge no commission at all. Moreover, no *Beat Inflation* investor will hold the same asset for long periods. He must therefore avoid being eaten up by commissions. Brokers will rarely recommend no-load funds, for the obvious reason that they collect no sales commission when they sell one. But many of the reputable funds frequently advertise in *The Wall Street Journal* and *Barron's*. Everybody is perhaps familiar with the no-load common stock funds, but the *Beat Inflation* investor should be acutely aware also of the existence of no-load funds that invest in short-term money market instruments, commodity contracts, gold and bonds. Some no-load money market funds are listed in Figure 18 on page 112 and some no-load stock funds in Figure 17 on page 103.

NOMINAL   An adjective to describe economic magnitudes when they are valued at the market prices of a particular period. Thus, nominal gross national product in the year 1974 was $1398 billion when evaluated at the market prices that prevailed in 1974. By contrast, REAL gross national product valued in dollars of 1958 purchasing power, was $824 billion. We use the word nominal mainly for contrast with REAL or with the INFLATION PREMIUM built into interest rates or wages. Thus, the nominal rate of interest is the market rate prevailing on a particular day, or for some average of days or months. A reading of *The New York Times* for Friday, December 20, 1974, revealed, for example, that the rate of interest obtainable on federal funds closed at 8⅞ percent on the preceding day. This was the nominal rate of interest obtainable on federal funds on December 19, 1974. People who suffer from the money illusion look at only nominal values. The *Beat Inflation* investor is acutely aware of the difference between nominal and REAL values.

Purchasing Power   The amount of goods and services that a currency can buy. The change in the purchasing power of the U.S. dollar is traditionally calculated by dividing a general price index into one (a single unit of dollars). Thus, if prices were to double in, say, ten years, the purchasing power of a dollar would be cut in half. The important questions are always about the change in purchasing power in a particular time period. In January 1974 the purchasing power of a dollar spent on the commodities that make up the wholesale price index had declined by 54 percent over the preceding ten years; the purchasing power of the dollar spent on the commodities making up the consumer price index had declined by 50 percent.

Rating of Debt Instruments   Before a major debt issue is brought to market the borrower seeks an opinion of its quality from independent experts whose judgment is trusted by the investment community. The best-known groups of credit-risk experts for publicly traded debt instruments are at Standard and Poor's and Moody's. A debt instrument has been rated when the expert's opinion of quality is quantified by a set of letters such as AAA, BBB, etc. Here are the Moody's and Standard and Poor's rating systems with respect to credit risk and what the agencies themselves say they mean.

RATINGS BY INVESTMENT AGENCIES

Moody's

Aaa	Best quality
Aa	High quality
A	Higher medium grade
Baa	Lower medium grade
Ba	Possess speculative elements
B	Generally lack characteristics of desirable investment
Caa	Poor standing; may be in default
Ca	Speculative in a high degree; often in default
C	Lowest grade

Standard & Poor's

AAA	Highest grade
AA	High grade
A	Upper medium grade
BBB	Medium grade
BB	Lower medium grade
B	Speculative
CCC-CC	Outright speculation
C	Reserved for income bonds
DDD-D	In default, with rating indicating relative salvage value

REAL (as in real income, real wealth, etc.)   Almost everyone who has taken a course in economics, as well as many people who have not, has heard of the Robinson Crusoe economy or the barter economy. Money had not yet come into existence in this primitive world that economists analyze. In this world, people traded directly what they produced for what other people produced. Adam Smith (no quotation marks) made a big to-do over the number of deerskins that a primitive man could get for a beaver pelt. He spent many pages in *The Wealth of Nations* analyzing the factors determining values in this direct kind of exchange. When modern economists, including ourselves, use the word real they conceptually go back to the barter economy. Thus, the real value of anything is what it can be bartered for. Your real income is the bundle of actual goods and services from Triscuits to tricycles that your work will buy. Real wealth is the actual goods and services that your net worth can buy, and so on. So that when you read the word real, keep the barter idea in mind. Because barter was awkward and time-consuming, productivity increased when man began to use money. Money makes exchanges far, far easier, but it creates problems because it makes it difficult for individuals to figure out what their income and wealth are really worth. People can always value their wealth and income in terms of dollars. The problem is that the purchasing power of the dollar itself keeps changing. Here the real concept helps. By expressing values of income, wealth or wages, for example, in real terms, these are corrected for changes in the value of the medium of exchange.

The government publishes numbers on real income; statisticians correct changes in money values for changes in purchasing power of money. For example, gross national product increased from $977 billion to $1398 billion between 1970 and 1974, or 43 percent. But prices increased by 26 percent over the same period. Accordingly, real gross national product, valued in 1958 dollars, increased from $722.5 billion to $823.9 billion, or 14 percent over the same period.

As it is with the economy as a whole, so it is with you. To find out the real increase in your income, you simply have to divide the change in your dollar income by the increase in prices. The same thing is true of any economic magnitude normally expressed in dollar terms—wealth, stock prices, bond prices, the value of the cash you hold.

Risk   Whenever an investor buys an asset he makes a best guess of what the rate of return to holding that asset will be. There is always a chance, however, that his best guess will be wrong. In fact, he is wrong at least to some degree almost all the time. Risk is a measure of the degree to which he can be wrong. The chances of being wrong are inherently bigger for some investments than for others. These assets are classified as risky. Investments can be ranged along a spectrum of risk. For debt instruments, for example, the least risky assets tend to be the short-term debt instruments of the U.S. government and highly rated corporations and banks. The most risky tend to be longer-term issues of low-quality companies. Conventional investment analysis has come up with some worthwhile rules for minimizing the risks involved in achieving a given investment goal. These rules, which include diversification, are discussed in Chapter 4.

Risk Premium   The difference between the return on the highest-quality and lower-quality security. It is measured numerically by the spread between the interest rates prevailing on the highest-quality issues and those prevailing on various classes of lower-quality issues. At the peak of the inflation cycle, the risk premium widens, creating excellent investment opportunities in lower-rated investments. (See Bond Rule 2.)

Return   The return on an investment is the total profit (or loss) realized from holding it. The return consists of two parts: one, the annual payment of interest, dividends, rent, etc.; the other, the capital gain (or loss) realized (or potentially realized) when the asset is sold. The sophisticated investor looks to total return, stressing neither interest nor dividends at the expense of capital gains, nor capital gains at the expense of interest or dividends. But remember, when you calculate your total return, make sure you look at everything on an after-tax basis. In the upper-income tax brackets the effective tax rate on interest and dividends is higher than it is on capital gains.

Spot Market   In the terminology of investments, Spot Market is used in contrast to *Futures Market*. Most markets are spot markets. The distinguishing characteristic of a Spot Market is that transactions take place at today's prices and delivery is made immediately. In a *Futures Market*, prices may be determined now, but delivery is made in the future, and at that time the spot price may be different.

Time Deposit   Another name for a savings account. It got the name because the law says that a bank can require advance notice if you want to withdraw your savings. Technically, *Certificates of Deposit* are Time Deposits.

TRADE-OFF   A term in vogue among economists these days. It is used to describe the amount of extra inflation that is necessary to knock down the unemployment rate. Or, alternatively, the amount of extra unemployment that results from knocking down the inflation rate. The world is suffering from high and volatile inflation because the trade-off exists only in policy makers' heads. It does not exist in the real world. The trade-off mentality leads policy makers to shift from fighting unemployment to fighting inflation with monotonous regularity. This creates the policy cycle, the monetary growth cycle, the inflation cycle and many rich *Beat Inflation* investors. (See Chapter 2.)

Treasury Bill   A short-term IOU issued by the federal government, generally considered to be the safest interest-bearing investment in the whole wide world. Treasury bills (T-Bills) are auctioned weekly, and when the yields on them go way up everyone lines up to bid for them, from little old ladies in tennis shoes from Dubuque to Arab sheiks from Kuwait with plenty of oil money. However, the major buyers of these instruments still are large institutional investors, such as commercial banks, insurance companies and corporate treasurers with cash to invest for short periods of time.

TREND (OR TREND RATE)   "Nature," as the philosopher William James once said, is "a blooming, buzzing confusion." This is certainly as true about economic data as about anything else. One way to reduce the confusion is to try to figure out how some economic magnitude—prices, wages or the money supply, for example—has been changing on average over a considerable period of time. Measures of how much these economic variables have been changing over time represent an estimate of the trend. Certain trend rates, in the money supply and the inflation rate for example, play a critical role in the *Beat Inflation* strategy.

VARIABLE RATE INSTRUMENT   Most debt securities pay a fixed number of dollars in annual income to those who are lucky (unlucky) enough to hold them. Thus, AT&T's 2⅝% bonds of 1986 promise to pay the holder $26.25 for each $1000 in par value until they mature in 1986. The yield on this bond changes only as a result of changes in its market price or because of default. In recent years, however, a type of debt instrument has emerged that pays a different number of dollars each year. The number of dollars in any given year depends on changes in either the inflation rate or some open-market interest rate. First National City Bank, New York, for example, has issued an IOU that will pay to the holder a higher number of dollars the higher the Treasury bill rate. Similarly, the First Pennsylvania Bank and Trust Company, a Philadelphia-based commercial bank, has a savings deposit that yields a higher rate of interest the bigger the increase in the consumer price index. All bank deposits and

IOUs paying different amounts of money to the holder each year are variable rate instruments. They are a phenomenon of a world of high and variable inflation. The time may be coming when the investor can issue variable rate IOUs of his own. This is what the variable rate mortgage that is now being discussed is all about.

Yield   The percentage that is derived by dividing the annual return from an investment by its purchase price. For example, if a $2000 investment in common stocks pays $100 in annual dividends, the yield is 5 percent. Current yield is a similar term derived by dividing annual return from an investment by its current price. For example, if those stocks you bought for $2000 now sell for $1000, your current yield is 10 percent rather than 5 percent. This is a fact from which you should take no satisfaction.

Books have been written about yield. What was once thought to be a straightforward concept is now recognized to contain a lot of hairy complexities. But if you are in the right assets for the particular stage of the inflation cycle, the difficulties of defining yield can be safely ignored because they become important only when an asset is held for a long period of time.

Meet the Authors of
The Beat Inflation Strategy

Roger Klein is Executive Director of the Public Securities Association and was an economist for Citibank and Argus Research Corporation. William Wolman is a Senior Editor of *Business Week* and has been a frequent contributor to the financial pages of *The New York Times*. Their Beat Inflation approach has been widely discussed and reviewed in *The Washington Post, Business Week, The National Observer* and *The Wall Street Journal*. But a satisfied reader got in the last word: "Fantastic!"